Me, Myself, & Lies

As women, we tend to do an awful lot of talking. Unfortunately, our thoughts and words do not always lead to blessing. Jennifer Rothschild has provided us with a reliable manual on how our words can bring life and health to the body, mind, and soul. This I know for sure: Jennifer has 20/20 heart vision.

Kathy Troccoli
singer, author, speaker

I am crazy about Jennifer Rothschild. She communicates warmth, humor, and provocative thought, all within a few moments of being with her. We have giggled together, prayed together, and had soulish conversations together. I leave her presence always wanting more.

I had the opportunity of having more with Jennifer as I read her new book, *Me, Myself, & Lies*. It too is filled with warmth, humor, and thought-provoking nourishment for our souls. She demonstrates how crucial it is that we kindly talk truth to ourselves. We come away uplifted and satisfied. I predict there will be countless thousands of her readers happily talking to themselves as they push their grocery carts, drive to work, or make their dinner. Soul talk will become the best epidemic to hit town. I recommend you catch it.

Marilyn Meberg
author and one of the original
Women of Faith speakers

For those of us that have perfected the art of self talk to the level of our own internal talk show, Jennifer's book offers sweet peace and *quiet* to our souls. Full of wisdom and depth, Jennifer is never afraid to get personal and honest; she writes like the wise and trusted friend she is.

Nicole Johnson
author and dramatist
with Women of Faith

All of us talk to ourselves. We tell ourselves what we believe, or what others have told us, about ourselves. Too often, we believe and feel things about ourselves that are untrue. We can change our false beliefs and feelings by replacing them with truth. Jennifer has learned how to do this, and her passion has led her to share it with others. This book is Jennifer's story, and it offers freedom and confidence for those struggling with habitual negative, degrading, and painful self talk. Her story can become your story.

Freda V. Crews
licensed professional counselor
host of *Time for Hope*

A woman's brain is designed by our Creator to masterfully handle language and to connect memories, words, and feelings in very powerful ways. As a result, a woman's conversations with others and with herself tend to be infused with emotion and meaning. As Jennifer Rothschild will clearly show you in this enthralling book, God's wonderful words to women and His spectacular design of women can, when warped by the enemies of a woman's soul, become a dangerous, disparaging, and destructive force. This invigorating book is a prescription for a renewal of joy and peace in a woman's heart.

Walt Larimore and **Barb Larimore**
authors of *His Brain, Her Brain*

ME, MYSELF, & LIES

JENNIFER ROTHSCHILD

HARVEST HOUSE PUBLISHERS
EUGENE, OREGON

ME, MYSELF, AND LIES

Copyright © 2007 Jennifer Rothschild
Published by Harvest House Publishers
Eugene, Oregon 97402
www.harvesthousepublishers.com

ISBN 978-0-7369-6011-3 (pbk.)
ISBN 978-0-7369-6012-0 (eBook)

The Library of Congress has cataloged the earlier edition as follows:
    Rothschild, Jennifer.
    Self talk, soul talk / Jennifer Rothschild.
        p. cm.
    ISBN 978-0-7369-2072-8 (pbk.)
    1. Christian women—Religious life. 2. Self-talk. I. Title.
    BV4527.R68 2007
    248.8'43—dc22

                              2007011901

Printed in the United States of America

17 18 19 20 21 22 23 24 25 / BP-KBD / 10 9 8 7 6 5 4 3 2

In loving memory of my precious grandmother,

Sarah Bragg Richbourg

December 24, 1915–November 28, 2006

Contents

FOREWORD

BY ROBIN MCGRAW

The night I spoke at the Women of Faith conference in Anaheim, California, all the speakers gathered in a small room for prayer. It's a tradition at these events—an incredibly awe-inspiring experience to be surrounded by motivational people just moments before heading onstage to share with tens of thousands of women what we hope will be powerful words.

"May God be with Jennifer," someone prayed. I didn't know who Jennifer was and why we were saying a special prayer for her. It turns out I was sitting next to her at that moment; she would soon inspire me and move me to tears, and she would become my dear friend. Most importantly, I would soon understand that God is most certainly with Jennifer—and with all those who seek Him. You will too after reading this exceptional book.

My message at that conference, as well as in my book *Inside My Heart* and regularly on my husband's TV show, *Dr. Phil*, is that we all have the choice to live the life we want, to live with passion and purpose every single day. It's not always an easy choice, but it is ours to make. Of course we are born into legacies we wish were different, we grow up with baggage that can weigh us down, and with every challenge we face as adults, we can all too easily become paralyzed with self-pity, doubt, insecurity, and other self-defeating emotions. That's why the key to living a joyful life is all in the choosing—a choice Jennifer Rothschild has made with the utmost dignity, optimism, and grace.

It's easy to forget that Jennifer has not been able to see since she was 15 years old because she never lets her disability define her. In fact, she only references that she is blind a handful of times in this book. She has *chosen*—my favorite word because we all have a choice—to make blindness her friend and to focus on all she has gained and continued to nourish as a result of losing her sight, including a keen self-awareness and unbending faith in God. These are only two of the gifts that Jennifer now uses to empower every one of us to live with vitality, freedom, wisdom, and peace.

In this book, Jennifer strikes the perfect balance between sharing her own experiences and citing Scripture to awaken us to the possibilities of our own lives. Hope and happiness are choices Jennifer has made, and now she offers the tools and insights for each of us to also make room for more goodness in our lives. Jennifer is a blessing in my life and in the lives of all those she touches. You're about to discover why. Enjoy!

Robin McGraw
Bestselling author of *Inside My Heart*

Part 1

THE LIFE-CHANGING POWER OF SOUL TALK

*When my words agree with God's
Word, I am free to be me.*

Do you talk to yourself? Oh, girl, I do! Most of the time, I keep it to myself, but there have been a few embarrassing times when I've had a full blown conversation right out loud! But right now, in this moment, on this page, I'm not talking to me. I'm talking to you. I'm so happy you picked up this book! You may have chosen it because you think you tell yourself lies. Or you may wonder what a thought closet makeover looks like. Or maybe you did my Bible study called Me, Myself, and Lies, and you want to refresh, review, and enjoy the new update.

Or you may have been one of those self-talking women who read my book *Self Talk, Soul Talk* about ten years ago. If so, this new book is an update of that classic content—including sneak peeks into more women's "thought closets." (If you're like me, you can't remember what you read back then anyway!) No matter the reason, ultimately you picked up this book because you too are a self-talking woman who wants to know what to say to yourself and, girl, we're about to figure that out!

We all have what I call a thought closet, and most of us need to clean it out once in a while. We need to dust off the shelves, throw some stuff away, and make sure we want to keep all that hangs there. Why? Because what we tuck away in our thought closets is what we wardrobe our lives with. In other words, the way you live is a reflection of the way you think.

As the saying goes:

> Sow a thought, reap an action.
> Sow an action, reap a habit.
> Sow a habit, reap a character.
> Sow a character, reap a destiny.

The life we long to live begins with our thoughts. If we want a change in our lives, it starts with a change in the way we think…in the way we talk to ourselves. Your life can be transformed by the life-changing power of soul talk. What is soul talk, and how does it work?

In these first four chapters, you'll discover that everybody practices self talk, but few of us actually take time to think about the things we say to ourselves. The process is so natural that we don't even notice it.

And there's the problem. We don't stop to consider whether the things we tell ourselves are even true. Amazingly, much of our self talk is false. It's based on lies that can keep us from entering fully into the lives God wants us to enjoy. But when we tell ourselves things that are true—when our words agree with God's Word—we can experience freedom like never before!

This kind of truthful self talk is what I call *soul talk*. It's speaking truth to the inner you—your soul.

Our self talk, soul talk is powerful. The words we say go straight to the core of our being. They shape the way we think about ourselves. They influence our emotions and our decisions. They resurface in our conversations with other people. They can spur us on to live meaningful, productive lives, or they can make us not even want to get out of bed!

So how can you make your self talk productive? How can you replace the lies you may have been telling yourself with truthful soul talk? Well, sister, God has made a way for you to make sure the words you say to your soul are the words He would say. And then you can be sure they are true!

What I put in my thought closet I will wardrobe my life with.

1

NOT SO WELL WITH MY SOUL

It is well with my soul.

That's been my story for years. I've spoken those words again and again. I've written about them. I've even sung them. As a speaker, writer, and sometimes-singer, I seem to gravitate to this same theme whether my audience is 50 business people in a hotel conference room or 5000 women in an arena. And I really mean it—it *is* well with my soul. These lyrics from a much-loved Protestant hymn echo the theme of my life story.

But here's the deal. The chorus demands that you boldly proclaim at the top of your lungs "It is well" no less than three times—whether you feel that way or not!

I wish I could count how many times I've stood and sung those words after speaking before an audience, only to sit right back down and feel a complete lack of wellness with my soul.

You should hear some of the unkind things I've said to myself.

You should have done a better job.

Listen to that speaker. She's SO much smarter than you.

Face it, girl, you'll never measure up.

Oh, my friend, I could go on and on. That's happened too many times to count. As a result of so many personal attacks—me against me—it has not always been so well with my soul! I've told myself so many untruths, and I more than half believed them. You know what I'm talking about, don't you? You don't have to be onstage to point that unforgiving microscope on your life, right?

It wasn't only when I was onstage. My steady flow of disapproving thoughts and self talk once formed a constant stream. I badgered, nagged, devalued, and said cutting words to myself. At times, all those dark, negative put-downs felt like a raging river, dragging me down until I thought I might drown in my own self-condemnation. At other times, they have felt more like a constant drip-drip-dripping. Not loud and demanding, just a steady trickle of poison, creating an acidic wash of pessimism running through my mind. "The mind is its own place," John Milton wisely observed, "and in itself, can make Heaven of Hell, and a Hell of Heaven."

Never Good Enough

As a child, I could not escape the idea that whatever I did just wasn't good enough. Can you relate? I was a good girl with huge perfectionist tendencies—and painfully self-aware. And all those you're-not-good-enough thoughts pooled into an estuary in my mind from which the bitter waters flowed.

During my teen years I changed a lot, and so did the content of my self talk. It got worse!

That's when I actually started calling myself names when I didn't measure up or when I made mistakes.

At the age of 15, I became legally blind due to a disease called retinitis pigmentosa. Even though I took that difficulty with grace and resolve, believe me, the extra challenges of the disability and the knowledge that blindness was inevitable brought even more opportunities for me to struggle with negative thoughts and destructive self talk.

You're never going to be independent.
You're so awkward.
People are staring at you.
Boys will never want to date you.

On and on it went. It was all about me, myself, and lies! By the time I'd made it through the decades of my twenties and thirties, I was swimming in a toxic ocean of accumulated self talk. All those years of faulty thinking and equally faulty self talking had begun to show up in bouts of frustration, sometimes pushing me to the ragged edge of despair.

I lacked confidence and struggled with insecurity. I wasn't unhappy or depressed all the time or miserable most days. Absolutely not. I got married and was blossoming professionally. I became a mom and pursued life with passion, curiosity, and honesty. But an unseen undertow was trying to pull me backward, denying me the chance of really feeling free. A battle was being waged in my mind, and I never even realized its impact at the time.

We grow so accustomed to our own self talk that we don't even recognize its corrosive nature and the damage we're inflicting on our own souls. It's just normal for us.

Normal like cancer.

The truth is, our self talk actually begins to shape the life we live, affecting our very destiny. *What you think and say to yourself will impact the music of your life.* The song I mentioned earlier begins with these lyrics:

When peace like a river attendeth my way,
When sorrows like sea billows roll,
Whatever my lot, Thou hast taught me to say,
"It is well, it is well with my soul."

Whatever your lot, do you want to be able to say it is well with your soul? I sure do. I know you do too. Knowing what to say to your soul is one of the most reliable ways to make sure it remains well. Words are extremely powerful—even the ones you speak to yourself.

Over the years, I have learned what to say when I talk to myself, and that has truly made all the difference in my life. After years of struggling beneath the weight of my own slander and lies, I have learned to speak truth to my soul.

It's what I call *soul talk.* And from this page forward, that's the term I will use most often in this book.

My Thought Closet

It all began early one morning as I wiped the sleep from my eyes. As the brain fuzz cleared, I was bombarded with a deluge of unexpected, unwanted quandaries and problems. Before my feet even hit the floor, I had scolded myself about the poor parenting job I was doing with my teenage son and had questioned whether my toddler was getting enough attention.

I hadn't intended to start my day with these thoughts.

What happened? I wondered.

Dragging myself to the kitchen to fix breakfast, I felt the old frustration rising within me. As I toasted some Pop-Tarts and scrambled some eggs, I continued to deliberate. *What's wrong with me?*

My oldest son left for school, and I sat at the kitchen table, sipping a cup of hot tea and trying to unknot a big tangle of emotions.

Was my brain simply an involuntary muscle, twitching and cramping, causing me to think on things that were not of my choosing? Why didn't I have control of the gray matter located beneath my color-treated hair and between my own pierced ears?

I seem to have a secret closet tucked somewhere in the hallways of my mind. A thought closet. And what I had been storing in that closet wasn't good at all: shelves and racks and bins full of hidden thoughts, secret insecurities, lies, illusions, and reminders of former failures. How did they get there? Why can't I get rid of them?

Without my consent, my mind keeps reaching into the dark

corners of that closet to retrieve the ugly junk I have inadvertently stored away over the years. The boxes have labels like these:

You're not good enough.
You're not the wife you could be.
You're not a good mom.
You should have done a better job.

One unsightly shelf was stacked high with bins full of junky feelings and beliefs…

It's all about me.
I can't do it; it's impossible.
I'll always be this way.
Nobody really cares.

Some things in life are only truly discovered through pondering, prayer, and a steaming cup of Earl Grey. My soul-talk revelation was one of them. As I questioned my seemingly helpless state, I felt as if God Himself reminded me that if I don't control my thoughts, my thoughts *will* control me. And the only way to get any kind of handle on those thoughts is to monitor what I tell myself.

Somehow, I had to stop my mind's reflex of continually rummaging through those boxes of ugly, ill-fitting thoughts and words. Or maybe I just needed to fill my closet with some more appealing, better-fitting self talk!

Hmmm…"Peace like a river" was about to be attending my way.

Let's Talk Soul Talk

Oh girl, we can be honest. We all talk to ourselves. Some of us have full-blown conversations—right out loud. Others of us just mutter silent phrases now and then. But we all engage in either destructive self talk or constructive soul talk.

Our *soul talk* can finally change the contents of our thought closets. If we want the right things on those shelves and in those bins, we have to tell ourselves right things. My faith has led me to the Bible to find what to say to my soul. And speaking the truths I've found in the pages of Scripture has turned my thought closet from a prison into an oasis of freedom! No sermons—just sensible soul talk!

Wherever you find people, you'll find all kinds of self talk—good and bad. And since the pages of Scripture are filled with the stories of real flesh-and-blood people, you'll see it there too. Both Deborah the prophetess and David the psalmist talked to themselves—and they weren't the only ones. Several other psalmists and even some New Testament characters were "caught on tape" having conversations with themselves. In fact, when many of them spoke, they knew very well they were addressing their own souls.

What did they say? What did they tuck away in their thought closets? Here's a sampling:

- "Awake, my soul" (Psalm 57:8).
- "My soul…put your hope in God" (Psalm 42:5,11; 43:5).
- "I have stilled and quieted my soul" (Psalm 131:2).
- "O my soul…forget not all his benefits" (Psalm 103:2).
- "Be at rest once more, O my soul" (Psalm 116:7).
- "March on, O my soul; be strong" (Judges 5:21).
- "Praise the LORD, O my soul" (Psalm 103:1; 104:1; 146:1).

Now that's what I call soul talk! In today's vocabulary, these seven soul-talk statements might sound a little like this…tune in, look up, calm down, look back, chill out, press on, and lift up.

Unlike David, Deborah, and the others, we don't usually make obvious "O my soul" pronouncements when we talk to ourselves. We use silent words instead. Some psychologists and neuroscientists have concluded that everybody maintains a continuous, ongoing silent dialogue, or stream of self talk, of between 150 and 300 words a minute. These are grouped into 45,000 to 51,000 thoughts each day. [1] Most of those thoughts are neutral or harmless, such as *Where did I put my keys?* or *I need to go to the cleaners today.*

But another small yet powerful percentage of such self-directed speech packs quite a punch. The thoughts can be accurate or inaccurate, constructive or destructive, right or wrong, and they matter a lot more than remembering to drop off your dry cleaning.

Our soul-talk thoughts seem to be etched into our brains as they travel neural pathways and carve out comfortable grooves for themselves along the way. Put less technically, we fill our thought closets one thought at a time, one silent word at a time, one utterance of soul talk at a time.

The thoughts that run through our minds become the inventory we store away in our closets. And out of that inventory we daily draw truth or error—powerful, life-shaping beliefs that go on to influence both our feelings and our actions. And the reality is, once in the closet...forever in the closet.

Our words are powerful. Especially the words we say to ourselves. That's why we need to take a peek into our own closets and see what's lining those shelves. And, through the pages of this book, I'll give you a glimpse into my thought closet and we'll also get a sneak peek into other women's thought closets. But, most importantly, I hope you will begin to take a good, hard look into your own!

Let's Sneak a Peek

After my most recent move, I vowed that I would never again buy clothes I wasn't totally in love with just because they were on sale. The reason? My closet was full of clothes I seldom wore but was hesitant to part with. Once something hung in my closet, I felt strangely attached to it and responsible for it. After all, I bought it. Even though I wouldn't dare wear those fuchsia and orange floral pants, they were mine. Once in my closet, forever in my life.

Our thought closets are much the same. They are crammed with everything we've placed there over the years; some of it is worthy and wonderful, but lots of it is ugly, outdated, out of line, and out of place.

Wise shoppers stock their closets with good wardrobe choices, and we must do the same with the things we say to our souls because each thought gets shoved in the closet until we recall it. We must speak truth to our souls because we seldom forget what we have stored away.

Isn't it funny that as we age, many of us can't remember the simplest things—like our children's names or why we left one room and walked into another? The older I get, I rarely get my boys' names correct on the first try. Most of my conversations with them start with "Clayton—I mean, Connor," or "Connor...uh, I mean, Clayton."

I've actually mixed together cake batter, poured it into the baking pan, and then returned to the kitchen half an hour later to check on it only to find that I placed it in the refrigerator instead of the oven.

We forget the simplest things, but when accessing our thought closets and their accumulated contents, our minds are like steel traps. We have the appalling ability to remember all the wrong things at all the wrong times. Like a finely tuned GPS, we can locate just the right memory of failure, the perfect insecurity, or the timeliest untruth—just when we don't need it most!

That's why we need to sneak a peek into our closets. Think about it. What hangs in yours? Does it supply you with truth? Is your thought closet full of all you need to live the life you desire? If not, don't fret, my friend. You can get control of those unprofitable thoughts in your closet.

In the coming chapters, you will see just how to do that.

Inventory Adjustment

It's time we take inventory. The stale contents of our overstuffed closets should not be the source of our musings. It's time to update the wardrobe. Now is your opportunity to fill your closet with timely, attractive truth with which you can clothe yourself: fashionable, well-fitting, freeing, and fabulous truth.

"Be transformed," St. Paul tells us, "by the renewing of your mind" (Romans 12:2).

Instead of drawing from a dilapidated closet, full of thoughts that just don't fit, we need a wardrobe jam-packed with healthy soul talk.

My friend, you are a reflection of the way you think. Wise King Solomon hit the nail on the head when he said, "For as he thinks within himself, so he is" (Proverbs 23:7 NASB). What you hang in your closet is what you will clothe yourself with. Your soul talk will affect who you are.

Because your thoughts strongly influence you, you can learn to govern them with some truthful soul talk. This will start you on the path of right thinking. It will lead you to unknotted, productive feelings and free you up to live the life you long for.

You may have occasionally laughed at people who talk to themselves, imagining that they were a few bricks short of a full load. Maybe—and maybe not! It actually all depends on what they were telling themselves! Those self talkers might be further ahead in the game of life than you might imagine.

When you speak truth to your soul, you'll live out the truth. Your soul talk really can help it become well with your soul.

Soul-Talk Questions to Ponder

1. What does the soundtrack of your self talk most often sound like—condemning, encouraging, or neutral?

2. How do you feel about the contents of your thought closet? Are the contents supplying you with what you need to live the life you desire?

3. Are you willing to try some soul talk from the Bible?

At the end of each chapter, take a moment to visit MeMyselfandLies.us to go a little deeper, have a little fun, and stay connected. If we're just getting to know each other, go to the website, watch a snippet of my story, and tell me yours.

Let the words of my mouth,
and the meditation of my heart,
be acceptable in thy sight,
O LORD, my strength, and my redeemer.
Psalm 19:14 KJV

2

RENEWING YOUR THOUGHT CLOSET

The older I get, the more often the words of my sweet, Southern grandmother echo through my thought closet.

"Mama" taught me a lot through her words and her life. I giggle now at one of her stern admonishments to me when I was just a little girl. With her small voice and Southern drawl, she would often say, "Honey, don't ever watch so-poppers."

As a young girl I vowed I would not—even though I had no idea what in the world "so-poppers" were. I did notice that each time my petite Mama preached her anti-so-popper doctrine, she was sipping a Coca-Cola and watching *Days of Our Lives* or *All My Children*.

Not until I was a young adult did I finally realize what she was actually warning me against. As thick as sweet Southern molasses, her Georgia accent had swallowed up the words *soap operas*.

That's great advice from my grandmother, but even greater wisdom comes from her favorite psalm. She quoted it to me often.

> Let the words of my mouth
> and the meditation of my heart
> be acceptable in thy sight,
> O LORD, my strength, and my redeemer (Psalm 19:14 KJV).

My precious Mama knew the power of words, and she wanted her granddaughter to know that power also. The writer of Proverbs tells us that the words of the wise are persuasive, that a person's words can be life-giving water, and that wise speech is rarer than gold and rubies.

Are we to take the Bible literally here? *More rare than gold or rubies?* How many rubies have you seen lying around lately? How often have you felt the weight of a 100-percent gold coin in the palm of your hand? I do believe Solomon is saying that truly wise and prudent speech is that rare. When you hear it, you know it, and you marvel.

Did you realize that your words could have such an impact?

In the pages of this book, my premise is that some of the most powerful words we utter are words no one else ever hears. They are the words we speak to ourselves.

Why do we speak them? Why, in particular, do we speak negative, nonproductive things to ourselves? We say them because they have found shelf space in our thought closets, and we find them near at hand in those moments when we are inclined to slander ourselves. These are the kinds of words that haunt us and plague us for years on end.

Label Makers

A man named Dennis confided one of the deepest hurts of his life. "I have three brothers," he told his friend Amy. "All the time I was growing up, when my father introduced us, he said my brothers' names, and then he always said, 'And this is our retarded son, Dennis.' It always made me feel so bad."

Dennis sobbed uncontrollably as the years of heartbreak washed over him once again. Amy tried to comfort him. She tried to explain that years ago, many people probably thought sharing this information with anyone was okay. And perhaps they thought that people with disabilities didn't really understand what was being said.

"So you see," Amy consoled, "they didn't know their words would hurt."

But Dennis had understood those words, and they cut him to the core. After decades, Dennis still heard the echo in his mind: *"My son is retarded."*

Each of us has things in our thought closets that we wish weren't there. We all have thrown things in without really considering where they came from or if they belong there.

Imagine being in a park and finding a filthy blouse over by the Dumpster. Could you ever see yourself picking it up, taking it home, and hanging it in your closet by your best little black dress?

In a sense, that's what we do. Only it's worse. We're not just taking a mucky piece of clothing and hanging it in a closet; we're taking dirty, ill-fitting words and storing them in the sanctity of our minds!

We have borrowed unbecoming beliefs from other people and hung them in our thought closets. We have grabbed clumsy considerations and careless characterizations and made them part of our wardrobe even when they didn't come close to fitting.

But we can refuse to let untruths and destructive words and thoughts occupy prime space in our minds' closets. Lies might come piled high in bags and bins, but we can refuse to open the door and place them on a shelf or hang them up. We can "hold them captive" until we determine whether or not they belong.

Keeping Watch at the Closet Door

A particular Scripture helped me as I began to take inventory of my closet, deciding what belonged and what didn't. The apostle Paul knew that the infant group of believers in the city of Corinth were bombarded with lots of information and that they had to decipher the truth from lies. To help them in this, he wrote a letter to the church and gave them great advice. He told them to be constantly "fitting every loose thought and emotion and impulse into the structure of life shaped by Christ" (2 Corinthians 10:5 MSG).

The King James Version translates Paul's phrase, "bringing into captivity every thought to the obedience of Christ." Regardless of the translation, the point is that you and I must take some control of our thoughts. We must train them to match up with truth. If we don't keep a hold on them, they will soon gain a hold on us.

Poor Dennis probably did struggle with an intellectual disability, but unfortunately, the carelessly spoken word *retarded* became a hurtful label. It made him different from his brothers—less regarded, less valued. The label continued to have the power to break his heart many, many years later.

If you have been labeled by some unfortunate words in the past (remember, these are words you could have spoken to yourself or repeated from others), such as *dummy, idiot, ugly, lazy, fatso,* or whatever (you fill in the blank), then you too know how those words can have a hold on you. Until you choose to bring that out-of-place label into the light and make it line up with truth, it will control you. Oh, friend, you don't have to live with those lying labels! Instead of wearing those destructive words as a label, choose now to label them with the truth.

So how do we do that? How do you hold your thoughts captive? How do you relabel? What does that look like in our daily lives? Here's an example.

Even during the writing of this book, I had a big silent conversation with myself. It began as I rode home from the post office in utter frustration and under lots of stress. I had carved out some time during a very busy week to travel 30 minutes downtown to apply for a passport. After waiting in a long line, I turned in my application and photo only to hear a lethargic and impatient clerk ask, "Where's your birth certificate? You can't get a passport without a birth cert—"

"Okay," I said. "I'll get it. I'll come back." The clerk let out an apathetic groan and yelled, "Next." He didn't say it, but in my mind, I knew what he was thinking: *Idiot.*

So as I rode home, that's what I said to myself. *Idiot. Why didn't you think of that? Now you have to come all the way back and see that unpleasant person again. Anybody knows you need a birth certificate. Idiot. Idiot. Idiot.*

Just as those wrong thoughts cascaded through my mind, I checked myself. I held my thoughts. As I did, I heard more clearly what I was saying. And I spoke truth to my soul instead.

Jennifer, I said firmly to myself, *you are* not *an idiot. That was a lie. You're just human, and humans make mistakes.*

I continued, *Remember, Jennifer, you are the workmanship of God. He doesn't make idiots.*

I was still frustrated, still upset by my mistake, but I was no longer held captive by destructive thoughts. Instead, I held those thoughts captive and made them agree with truth. Instead of letting *idiot* into my thought closet, I refused it entry. In fact, I guarded the door. And if it happened to slip in, I relabeled it and put it back on the shelf, filed under *workmanship of God* and *human.*

Holding thoughts captive and making them agree with truth requires that we have the wisdom to even recognize truth. Yes, wisdom is the watchman at the door of our thought closets. Speaking wisely is essential when you speak to yourself.

When you talk to yourself, do you choose wise words? Are they words God would put His loving stamp of approval on? Are they like life-giving water, or do they drain away your vitality, leaving you parched, dry, and arid?

Words matter. We cannot risk speaking untruths to ourselves because of the strong likelihood that we will believe them.

The average woman uses approximately 25,000 words a day. That only includes the ones researchers can hear and record. As you know, we speak a heap more that no one but us ever hears. We speak those words in silence to ourselves, and we quickly stow them away in our thought closets.

So how do we know what belongs there? How do we apply wisdom and train ourselves to recognize truth and speak truth to our souls?

What Does Truth Sound Like?

Listen with me to the One who is full of grace and truth, and consider the way Jesus used words. He demonstrates what wisely spoken truth sounds like. A brief account in the Gospel of Luke gives us a clue.

Jesus had come back home to Nazareth for a visit, and He stood in the synagogue on the Sabbath to teach. Dr. Luke tells us in verse 22 of chapter 4 that after Jesus finished speaking, "All spoke well of him and were amazed [or astonished] at the gracious words that came from his lips."

His words were gracious.

A few verses and several cities later, we see Jesus again in a synagogue on the Sabbath. This time He is in Capernaum. The people "were amazed at his teaching, because his message had authority."

His words were powerful.

So Jesus was known not only for His gracious words but also for His authoritative speech. Isn't that what we seek in our own soul talk? The truth is always authoritative and gracious. Authoritative words should never be harsh, and gracious words should never be without power. If our words reflect God's words, even *we* will be amazed and astonished at the One who speaks truth to and through us.

Are the words you speak to yourself gracious? Are they kind? Or are they harsh? Do your words condemn you? Are the words you use based on the power of Scripture? Do you tell yourself the truth without condemning yourself when you blow it?

"What difference does it make?" you may ask. "It's just me. No one else is hurt. No one is listening." But that's just the point—someone *is* listening. *You* are listening. And you matter. You are loved and created by God, and when you hurt yourself with ugly words, you not only hurt yourself, you hurt the One who loves you. The words you say to yourself—both true and false—have the same impact as words you speak to others or that they speak to you. So, sister, if you wouldn't talk that way to someone you dearly love, don't talk to yourself that way either. It's not full of grace—it's full of condemnation.

I had an interesting conversation with a "professional talker" about this very thing. Marilyn Meberg is a licensed therapist, an author, and a professional speaker. Take a sneak peek into Marilyn's thought closet as she described her own self talk to me.

> **JENNIFER:** Do you ever speak to yourself with self-condemnation? What if you do something stupid? Do you ever say, *Marilyn, you knucklehead!*
>
> **MARILYN:** (Laughs) A million times.
>
> **JENNIFER:** But not to the extent that it's a real problem?
>
> **MARILYN:** (Laughs even louder) *Of course* to the extent that it's a problem! But when I speak to myself that way, sometimes I need to hear that. Sometimes I've done a dumb thing, a tactless thing, something that is lacking wisdom. And I will chastise myself, and I need to hear that sometimes. It's like a parent has to discipline a child. I discipline myself. *Now Marilyn, you could avoid that next time, if you would just...*
>
> **JENNIFER:** So you *counsel* yourself?
>
> **MARILYN:** I take myself into my office and I have a chat. And when I come out of the office, I either want my money back, or I'll say, *You know, that was good.* That's constructive, not condemning, though. As you know, there are some levels of self-condemnation that are damaging.
>
> **JENNIFER:** How do you know the difference?

MARILYN: Oh, sometimes I need the correction. Sometimes I need the discipline. Sometimes I need to own the truth. That's instruction. That's good for me. That builds me up. But when I feel condemned, like I'm not good enough, that's not instructive. That's destructive. Instruction brings life, condemnation brings destruction.

Wise, truthful words are never harsh or unkind. They are gracious. Wise and truthful words are never wimpy or without power. They have authority. Even the hard truths we speak to ourselves should not be condemning. They should build us up. Like Marilyn, we can and should counsel ourselves with the truth. But, my friend, if you counsel yourself harshly, you too need to get your money back.

Proverbs 18:21 says, "The tongue has the power of life and death." That's pretty weighty. Life and death? Yes, my friend. Your words can contribute to your vitality, or they can begin your demise. They can build up, or they can tear down. That's why they must be gracious and authoritative.

Remember, the wise proverb is not reserved only for the words you speak to others; your tongue has power and influence over you.

So how do you wield your influence? Are your words gracious and yet based on the authority of Scripture? I am quite sure I would not tolerate someone else speaking to me with the kind of words I have used when speaking to myself. You know what I mean. If my husband, Phil, ever called me an idiot because I spilled coffee on his newspaper, I would be crushed and explode with indignation. Yet *idiot* is the word I most frequently called myself when I made a similar blunder. And it still can come to my lips if I'm not careful.

Listen: The *same indignation* should fire up when I speak those grave-digging words to myself. Clearly, *idiot* is not gracious or based on the authority of Scripture. It is not instructive. It is destructive. I can't afford to hang that kind of untruth in my closet, and neither can you. It's too easy to retrieve and too hard to relinquish.

As with all writers, I'm very aware of "word counts"; I need to know if I've written too much or too little. As a woman prone to talking to myself, I need to be just as aware that my words—the words I say to myself—*count*. And so do yours. Perhaps we would all benefit from measuring and contemplating our words the same way a writer does before the stroke of her pen. You see, we all write on the tablets of our own minds when we speak to ourselves.

Since you also have the tendency to mutter silent words to yourself, remember that what you say matters because, sister, you matter. The next time you gear up to spout off some choice words to your soul, pause and consider the words of Paul: "Let your conversation be gracious and attractive so that you will have the right response for everyone" (Colossians 4:6 NLT).

Hear me, my friend. "Everyone" includes *you*. You need the right answer tucked away in your thought closet. *Idiot* is not the right answer. *You should have done that as well as your sister does* is not the right answer. Only words that lead to life and vitality convey the right answers.

So in your conversation with yourself, begin to take notice. Are you speaking truth? Do the words you use to influence your thoughts bring life and vitality?

Cleaning out an overstuffed closet is probably not your idea of a fun afternoon. It seems easier to just close the door (if you can) and ignore all that unsightly and useless stuff. But when it comes to your thought closet, that stuff will own you as long as you own it. It's essential that you start to do some sorting—some inventory assessing—a little at a time.

Once you identify what doesn't belong in your closet, you can begin to hold thoughts captive at the closet door and relabel what is already stored in there.

At this point, you might be asking if you can get rid of what's in your thought closet. After asking several experts and really pondering that question, here is my conclusion:

No.

We probably never completely erase old memories, forget old thoughts, or wipe away former self talk. Those things are simply there, and depending on what we do with them, they add or subtract to the quality of our lives. Our closets are permanently lined with all we have placed there, enhancing or corrupting our attitudes and actions.

You can't remove those hurtful thoughts, words, and memories, but by the power of God, you can drain them of their potential control over you.

Only One is truly capable of forgetting, and that is God Himself. He is a perfect forgetter; we are imperfect forgetters. Through the power of His Spirit living within us, we can relabel the items in our thought closets. That's how we update the old wardrobe that hangs there. We replace the lie with the truth, and we relabel the old with the new. And that's soul talk.

Eventually, those old self-talk lies will be so buried under layers of wisely spoken truth that you will be wearing the wardrobe of freedom.

Bring it on.

Soul-Talk Questions to Ponder

Before we go on, check out your closet.

1. What sits on the shelves and hangs out in the furthest corners? What's the first fragrance you smell when you open the closet door?

2. What are the top five thoughts you have about yourself? How do they influence your behavior and feelings?

3. Are the contents of your thought closet based on truth or lies?

4. Are you a name caller? If so, find a new name to use when you are tempted. Remember my post office example—I called myself *the workmanship of God* rather than *idiot*. In other words, refrain from the old words and rephrase with new words.

For tips and resources to help you with your thought closet, visit MeMyselfandLies.us. You'll find more interviews with women talking about what's in their thought closets.

A SNEAK PEEK INTO LAURA STORY'S THOUGHT CLOSET

I've never been more motivated to wear waterproof mascara than after I listened to Laura Story sing and play her Grammy Award-winning song, "Blessings," at a conference where I was speaking! I was so impacted by her story and the words of her song that I cried—not cute girly cried…I mean gasping and snotty cried—through every verse and chorus! Those tears began a beautiful friendship. And since I knew such moving and deep lyrics of the song had to come from a well-examined thought closet, I asked her if she ever struggled with bad self talk or if it was easy for her to keep her thought closet full of truth.

• • •

"I've been known to let destructive self talk bounce around in my head, but I'm learning to take every thought captive. To focus on my past sin is diminishing God's grace in my life, or more importantly, what Jesus endured to deal with my sin. There is no condemnation from God because of Jesus' work on the cross, so when I hear those accusations and reminders of past failures, I can immediately know that voice isn't God's.

"I've learned I have to fill my mind with Scripture.

"If I fill my mind with romantic comedies every night on Netflix, I will begin to believe that the perfect guy is the answer to life's problems. If I spend hours and hours on Pinterest, I will start to think that the perfect-looking home or the most creative kid's birthday party (or whatever people look at on Pinterest) is the answer to life's problems. Don't get me wrong. There's nothing wrong with any of these things; it's when we spend more time hearing what the world has to say about life than hearing what God has to say. And I am the most guilty of this! Ever since I've been a mom, it's been a struggle to get up early enough to spend time in His Word. I try hiding in my closet, but the kids seem to always find me! But I'm still fighting for it, writing a verse or two on a sticky note on my bathroom mirror and even reading my kids' short gospel storybooks! Because ultimately I know that the best thing I can do as a wife and a mom is to have a thought closet full of truth."

*I refuse lies and replace
them with truth.*

3

CHOOSING
WISE WORDS

As a little girl on my way to church each Sunday, I rode with my family past a beautiful Catholic church. It was stately and ornate, and it didn't look like *my* church at all, and it always caught my eye.

Then came the day when it amazed me beyond words.

As a child I could see well, so colors, architecture, and even signage always captured my attention. So you'll understand my astonishment when my eyes landed on an ordinary street sign planted in the parking lot of this extraordinary church.

It read Angle Parking Only.

I was only about six or seven years old, and I evidently wasn't the best reader so I thought it had read *Angel* Parking Only.

I was overwhelmed with wonder that the Catholics had angels attending their services. Did the Methodists or Baptists or Lutherans? I had certainly never seen any at my church!

What's more, were they such expected guests at that church that they even had reserved parking? We boring Baptists had only humans attending our services—and the only reserved parking spot we had was for our pastor. But the Catholics had shiny medals, cool prayers, and now, angels in the parking lot!

I do remember that I became a little deflated and confused when I glanced through the angel parking area and noticed that the celestial beings drove such average vehicles. *An angel in a '64 Datsun? Really? I would have expected at least a Rolls Royce from heaven!*

Not until many years later did I realize my spelling gaffe. It was kind of fun thinking angels had places to park at the Catholic church, but I was wrong.

I'm not saying that angels never attend the services there. Who knows where their duties take them? But most likely, they don't drive Datsuns and they don't need reserved parking spots.

My thinking was based on a faulty assumption.

I fear that I've done the same thing many times throughout my life. I've operated under faulty assumptions based on wrong thinking in other, far more consequential areas.

When I was in college, I had some faulty assumptions. As a result, I filled my closet with lots of wrong thinking. Thoughts like *No matter how hard you try, you surely could have done better.* My assumption was that my worth was measured by how well I performed. Does that sound like a faulty assumption to you?

As a young wife, I brought my share of faulty assumptions into our marriage. I had lots of ill-fitting outfits in my thought closet. I had chosen to clothe myself with wrong thinking. Those misguided thoughts grew into unrealistic expectations, and I couldn't understand why my husband didn't get it! How could he be so insensitive?

I entertained thoughts like *If he really valued me, he would pick up his clothes and lower the toilet seat.* I thought that if Phil did something I didn't like, he did it because he didn't care about me. When he handled things differently than I would have, I thought his priorities were out of line. I assumed that it was all about me. Does that sound like a faulty assumption to you? And does that sound familiar?

We live by our assumptions, our beliefs about the way things are. We often aren't even aware of such ideas until we do a little self-examination. Our thoughts and our actions flow from our assumptions.

Root and Fruit

Simply put, our assumptions are the root, and our thoughts are the fruit. The root of wrong thinking is always a faulty assumption. The root of right thinking is always an assumption based on truth.

Suppose you had just landed on our planet and you encountered a lush plantation, thick with trees. You would certainly be curious about the different varieties, right? How would you determine the kind of trees you saw?

The fruit.

Yes, as an alien tree examiner you could dig down to cut a sample from the root system or perhaps take some kind of core sample from deep within the living wood. But the most practical way to figure out what kind of tree you were looking at (especially if your alien invasion was on a tight schedule) would be to examine its fruit.

So what is your fruit? Are you hypersensitive with other people—as I was with Phil? Do you constantly interpret other people's words and actions as personal attacks?

The fruit of hypersensitivity grows from the root of pride and an unhealthy degree of self-absorption. The faulty assumption is the root; the wrong thinking is the fruit.

Here's another fruit. During my college years, I was paralyzed by the notion that nothing I did was good enough. Do you ever think that way? If your fruit of perfectionism has matured, you may place those same unrealistic demands on the people you love.

The fruit of perfectionism springs from the root of low self-esteem or insecurity. The faulty assumption is the root; the wrong thinking is the fruit.

You don't simply become hypersensitive or perfectionistic without some faulty assumptions nourishing those fruits. Your fruit is a direct result of your roots. And changing the fruit is impossible without changing the root.

That implies a little digging, doesn't it?

So, my friend, it's up to you to determine the assumptions from which you operate. Are they true? Or are they faulty?

At this point, it isn't so important how you came by the faulty assumptions you now possess. I'm simply encouraging you to cut them off at the root. Sister, it's time to grab the ax! Sometimes we just need to call them what they are: damaging, ill, and unhealthy.

Calling something what it is helps you identify it and see it more clearly. It allows you to see it for what it is. If your root is deep in the soil of your life—tangled and choking you—you may need to get professional help so your fruit will blossom with new life. But if and when you are able, choke that root yourself with the truth. That's what I've done. I kept confronting the root every time I tasted the fruit.

When I reacted with hypersensitivity or defensiveness to Phil, I checked the root. Was I operating out of a faulty assumption? My answer was usually yes. Phil wasn't devaluing me in a moment of messiness or forgetfulness. His thoughts weren't even about me when he left the toilet seat up. (I guess I'm glad for that on some level.)

You begin to experience freedom when you discover your own root. You learn to choose your own fruit more wisely. We gain knowledge and understanding by examining ourselves, trying, learning, and even failing. We jiggle the root. We examine the fruit.

You are too valuable and life is too important to risk living by faulty assumptions. That's why I recommend making our roots strong, fertilizing them with thoughts that will produce healthy fruit: wise and truthful soul talk. To paraphrase King Solomon, may each of us trust in the Lord with *all* our hearts and lean *not* on our own understanding.

I want the assumptions I make to be wise and true, and I know you do too. Before we start looking at the soul talk in David's and Deborah's closets, let's consider how to wear it wisely.

Ways to Wisdom

Have you ever woken up mad at a friend or your spouse after a bad dream where he or she misbehaved? *How could he do such a thing? How could she say that? There must be SOME truth in it.*

After some time, the morning fog lifts from your brain, and you realize it was all in your mind. But the strange thing is that it feels so real, doesn't it? That's what living out a false assumption is like. It feels so real. But that doesn't mean it's right or true.

Have you ever made assumptions based on a misunderstanding or on wrong information? If so, let me give you three surefire ways to gain the wisdom you need to recognize truth, right assumptions, and healthy fruit.

Request Wisdom

First of all, ask God for wisdom. He won't begrudge you for needing knowledge. You won't get a black mark for imagining that angels have reserved parking at Catholic churches. The apostle James tells us, "If any of you lacks wisdom, he should ask God, who gives generously to all without finding fault, and it will be given to him" (James 1:5).

This isn't meant to be weirdly spiritual or complicated. It really is as simple as asking for wisdom and trusting that you will receive.

Our sons developed an odd habit when they were each about two years old. Whenever the phone rang, it signaled them to need me really badly. They could have been totally occupied, happy, and distracted until the phone rang. But when it did, they inevitably whined, got hurt, needed something, or simply wanted to be held. Something in the ring signaled a virtual meltdown in my kids.

One day, my publisher made a surprise phone call to our home. Trying to sound as if he were the most important person in my life at that moment, I attempted to hush Connor while he pulled on my leg. "Sucker, Mommy. Sucker, Mommy," he insisted. Because he asked, and because I knew the call was going to be a long one, I pulled a brand-new bag of Tootsie Pops I had purchased for Halloween out of the cabinet. I yanked it open and turned it upside down.

Like confetti at a parade, multicolored lollipops fell all over the kitchen floor. I smiled as big and approvingly as possible at Connor and mouthed, "Have fun." I then hid in the closet to finish my phone call.

The point is, he asked, and I answered.

Not just meeting minimal requirements, I gave liberally. That's how God is when He responds to our request for wisdom. He doesn't just meet minimal requirements. He gives liberally. He turns the bag upside down. He lavishes us with wisdom that will benefit us and those around us.

God made getting wisdom as simple as asking for it. Just as simply as a child asks for a lollipop or as simply as I ask my husband to "please pass the potatoes," we can ask God for wisdom. Amazing! And we receive an overflowing supply.

King Solomon echoed this thought: "For the LORD gives wisdom, and from his mouth come knowledge and understanding" (Proverbs 2:6). So, my friend, before you read on, ask God for wisdom, and trust Him to provide. Ask and you shall receive.

Revere God

You can also receive wisdom by choosing to reverence God. The book of Proverbs tells us, "The fear of the LORD is the beginning of wisdom, and knowledge of the Holy One is understanding." [1]

To fear the Lord doesn't mean to be deathly afraid of Him. No, He is good and kind. But He is also just and worthy of our highest regard and respect. To fear the Lord means we reverence Him.

It means to show deference and respect. It's acting toward God as if we were approaching a king who invited us into his royal chamber. We would be keenly aware of his high position, especially compared to our lowly one.

It means we regard God more highly than we regard ourselves. We esteem His truth more highly than we esteem our perceptions of truth. To fear the Lord means holding His knowledge and truth in higher regard than our own.

Examine your own heart and mind. Do you fear the Lord? Whose truth do you elevate most highly in your life? Yours, our culture's, or God's? Until you reverence God most highly in your life, until you acknowledge that He is the standard of truth, you will never experience Him as the ultimate source of truth—and you will never find true wisdom. Take a moment to reconcile those thoughts with your own. You will discover the wisdom you need when you choose to revere God.

Receive Counsel

You will also gain wisdom through counsel. Once again, the book of Proverbs advises us that "wisdom is with those who receive counsel," and "the wise of heart will receive commands." [2] When we walk with wisdom, it will wear off on us.

I was sitting in the green room before speaking at the Anaheim Women of Faith Conference. After a little small talk, I told Patsy Clairmont I was writing a book about what to say when you talk to yourself. After she uttered an interested *hmmm,* I popped the question. "Do you talk to yourself? And if you do, what do you say?"

In typical Patsy fashion, what followed was an articulate, well thought-out, fully lived-out answer. She only got a few phrases into it when I stopped her and asked, "Can I record this?"

So what follows is our conversation. Just pretend you are listening in as I get some wise counsel from a wise guide. By the way, Patsy told me she does talk to herself, and when she does, she sounds like a cheerleader.

JENNIFER: So when you talk to yourself, it's as a cheerleader?

PATSY: Absolutely, because it's my tendency to be extremely critical, especially of myself. In fact, I'm far harder on myself than I am on others.

JENNIFER: When did you figure that out—that you were being overly critical and telling yourself untruths? And how and when did you make a disciplined choice to stop?

PATSY: Well, I had so many people saying things to me that were in conflict with what I was saying to myself. One of us had to be wrong! So when I had more and more people saying the same positives to me, and my words were all negative, I had to stop and say, *Everyone can't be wrong. Do I trust their judgment? And do I think they are wise? Am I willing to receive that what they are saying is truth? If I am, then I have to change the messages in me.*

JENNIFER: So do those old messages still pop up?

PATSY: Every now and then.

JENNIFER: And do you know what prompts them?

PATSY: Well, it could be a sense of failure. Maybe if I did something that didn't work out as well as I had hoped. Suddenly I feel myself cascading down and that old critical spirit coming in, passing judgment on myself. And I have to ask myself, *What would I say to another person—to my friend—who had made the same mistake?* I would say, "You can't do that to yourself. You cannot believe that because the enemy is a liar and a thief and he comes in to set a lie in place and steal your joy."

So I have to deliberately go against such negative thoughts. One thing I've done for many years is a kind of three-step approach: *Refuse* things that are inaccurate, unkind, or unedifying; *replace* them with what is good, pure, and just; and then *repeat* that process for as long as it takes to bring my thoughts under control.

JENNIFER: That's fabulous. And that's worked for you?

PATSY: It's been exceedingly beneficial.

JENNIFER: And Patsy, it shows—it shows in the way you live.

Did you notice that Patsy benefited from the wise guidance of others? The counsel of other people helped her gain mastery over her own damaging self talk. And now you and I are the beneficiaries of the wisdom she gained.

Sometimes we just need to listen to others, learn from their mistakes and experiences, and recognize that others struggle the same way we do. Other people can teach us a lot if we'll take the time to listen.

Do you have a wise guide? Do you have someone you can walk with in order to gain wisdom? Maybe you are a guide, and you will continue to gain as you continue to give. In fact, my hope is that you can gain wisdom as you continue to read this book.

I'd like to walk with you down the path I've traveled and share the truth I've unraveled. I believe with all my heart that you will benefit from what I've learned on my personal soul-talk journey.

You will become well acquainted with wisdom when you simply request it, reverence God, and receive wise counsel. When you do, wisdom will become one of your best friends.

> Say to wisdom, "You are my sister," and call understanding your intimate friend (Proverbs 7:4 NASB).

I love that. If wisdom were truly your sister, what would she say to you on a casual morning walk along the river? If understanding actually happened to be your BFF, what would she say to you in a gut-honest conversation at a corner table in your favorite café? You can count on one thing. You wouldn't want to miss a single word.

The Wealth of Wisdom

> Wisdom is more valuable than gold. [3]
> Wisdom will refresh you as a bubbling brook. [4]
> Wisdom will bring healing to your life. [5]
> Wisdom will be pleasant to your soul. [6]
> With wisdom, your sweetness of speech increases. [7]
> The wise will inherit honor. [8]
> Wisdom grants you a future, and your hope will not
> be cut off. [9]
> Wisdom helps you understand your way. [10]
> Using wise words will protect you. [11]
> Wisdom makes you strong. [12]
> To get wisdom is to love your own soul. [13]

And wouldn't you just know it—wisdom helps you know what to say when you talk to yourself!

> A wise man's heart guides his mouth,
> And his lips promote instruction (Proverbs 16:23).

Wow. My friend, if you sprinkle the roots of your life with the wealth of wisdom, you will begin to see beautiful, healthy fruit blossom. To speak wisely to your soul will shrivel some of those old, sick roots and nourish the good roots that may be struggling.

Be patient with yourself. Roots are strong, but with wisdom, you are stronger. Applying the strength of truth to your faulty assumptions will help choke the life out of your bitter and sour fruit. And that, my friend, is a very good thing.

Soul-Talk Questions to Ponder

1. What are the fruits in your life you wish you could get rid of?

2. What are the roots from which those fruits grow?

3. What practical things can you do to attack the root so the fruit will die?

4. Remember what Patsy said: refuse, replace, and repeat for as long as it takes. What's your "fear factor"—do you fear God, reverence Him? If you struggle with this, get to know the God of the Bible. Read Psalm 23 and the Gospel of John to get started. Ask Him to reveal Himself in your life.

For tips and resources to help you with wise soul talk, visit MeMyselfandLies.us. You'll also find a fear-factor assessment and see fun pictures of me and Patsy Clairmont.

My soul talk can turn feelings of fear into actions of faith.

4

SPEAKING TRUTH
TO YOUR ISSUES

I don't know her name. Outside of heaven, no one does. But I have seen inside her thought closet, and after a quick peek I'm convinced we have a lot in common.

First of all, like me, the woman talked to herself. I like her already. And second, she had issues. Me too!

Maybe you've got some issues too? I imagine that we are all self-talking women with more than a few issues! Oh, sister, we have more issues than hours in the day to deal with them: illness, financial troubles, insecurities, relationship conflict, fear, sadness. Our thought closets are stuffed full of problematic stuff.

This woman had a single, insurmountable issue, and she had endured it for 12 long years. It had challenged her physically, strained her emotionally, drained her financially, and ostracized her socially.

That's what our issues do. They complicate everything. They challenge us, drain us, isolate us, and perplex us. That's one of the reasons we talk to ourselves. But we'd better be sure we're telling ourselves the right things or our issues will multiply, and we'll be in over our heads.

• • •

I can't imagine how she mustered the courage to leave home and do what she did.

She must have heard rumors of the gentle Healer—stories about the wonders that seemed to follow Him everywhere He went. Stories about His incredible power to heal with a word, with a touch.

When she learned Jesus was actually approaching her village, she began to watch for Him—not casually, but as if her life depended on it. As it turned out, finding Him wasn't that hard—not with the throng of people at His heels wherever He turned. Finding a place where He would pass by, she pressed her way through the crowd and found a position at the front.

And then…there He was. Just a few yards away from her, walking purposefully with Jairus, the leader of the synagogue. He walked right by her—close. Almost close enough to…

Just that quickly, the Teacher walked on by. Would she ever be this close to Him again? It was her last chance! Suddenly lurching forward, she did the unthinkable.

She reached out. She touched Him.

• • •

A Desperate Moment

The Gospel writer Mark told this woman's poignant story. For more than a decade, she had experienced the pain and embarrassment of a blood flow no physician could heal. That most likely meant that she couldn't get pregnant, and that alone was an utter heartbreak for a first-century Jewish woman—actually, for any woman who dreamed of becoming a mother. To add to her misery, she was destitute from years of medical expenses.

Mark summarizes her despair in one telling sentence: "She had suffered a great deal under the care of many doctors and had spent all she had, yet instead of getting better she grew worse" (Mark 5:26).

Her "issue of blood" (KJV) created a load of other issues. The same is true for you and me. We find ourselves with one defining circumstance in our lives that becomes the headwaters from which many other issues originate and flow.

Being overweight, for instance, invites low self-esteem, shaky confidence, or perhaps poor health. Maybe you grew up hearing and believing insulting messages, such as "You aren't good at anything," or "Your dad and I never planned you; you were just an accident." If you've endured defining words like those at some point in your life, you might battle with issues of self-worth or depression.

For me, blindness is a circumstance that opens the door to a ton of other bewildering issues. One of the biggest daily realities I face is the stress of not being able to drive, read, or enjoy independence. And stress, as you know, can morph into monster issues, like anger, isolation, or an identity crisis.

Our issues come with accessories that take up room in our thought closets. And once in, always in. An issue in itself! A new issue on the shelf!

So what are we to do? Is a steady diet of healthy soul talk really enough to remedy our issues? How did the woman with the "issue" of blood cope for all those years?

There comes a time when you must speak a word to your soul that prompts action resulting in healing. Stay tuned. You might be surprised by what I mean.

Her action? She reached out her hand and touched Jesus.

Before we speed by this, let's pause to reflect on the risks of her radical deed. In first-century Israel, a woman simply didn't touch a man in public. It wasn't done—especially when he wasn't her husband. And even more so if the man were a rabbi, a teacher of the sacred Law.

We aren't talking about bad taste or political incorrectness here. *It was illegal.* A woman probably wouldn't even dare *speak* publicly to a rabbi.

To make matters even more socially unthinkable, she was unclean by Jewish legal standards. Yes, when someone was bleeding, she was unclean and had to be isolated. For an unclean woman to reach out to touch a devout teacher of the Law was inconceivable. In our more relaxed contemporary culture, we can't begin to imagine the risk this woman took. Her plan cut across the grain of every social, political, and religious boundary. It was an act of utter desperation—just a quarter inch away from complete despair.

So how did she find the courage to act in a way that was so radical, so countercultural? Matthew gives us a clue when he notes, "She kept saying to herself, 'If I can only touch his coat, I will get well.'" [1]

There it is: *She talked to herself.*

She confronted her issue and practiced some soul talk. (And she hadn't even read this book!) She told herself that if she touched Him, she would be healed. She encouraged, counseled, and advised her soul.

Her words prompted her action—she extended her arm from the middle of a crowd to brush her fingers across the hem of His robe.

With that merest touch, a brush of homespun cloth across her fingertips, her great need ran head-on into His limitless provision. In that instant, her courage met His compassion. Her hope met His holiness, and she was healed. Scripture says, "The woman, knowing what had happened to her, came and fell at his feet and, trembling with fear, told him the whole truth" (Mark 5:33).

Few biblical stories do more to validate my own soul talk than this story about this hurting woman. Researchers and psychologists today might say she was a great example of the power of positive self talk. Perhaps she was. But the most important thing to note here isn't that she talked to herself. It's what she told herself that matters. She didn't mouth a bunch of happy talk or a mantra of feel-good phrases. She spoke words of wisdom and truth to her soul.

Counseling ourselves to act upon truth, coaching ourselves, and cheering ourselves on to make good choices—these are both healthy and wise. Wise soul talk pushes us over the edge to help us overcome our issues. In this story, the woman with the hemorrhage clearly benefited by telling herself that she would be healed if she touched Jesus' robe.

Though her words themselves held no power, their message did. Her soul talk turned feelings of fear into actions of faith. Her desperate act impressed Jesus so much that He responded to her.

"Daughter, your faith has healed you."

Now, my friend, what I am about to say next is one of the most important statements of this book. Let these words sink in.

Jesus never said her soul talk made her well. He said it was her *faith*. Her *faith* invited healing. Her soul talk contributed to her faith, but it didn't replace her faith. She spoke truth to her soul in the same way you and I need to speak truth to our souls.

By faith we receive truth. By faith we believe truth. And by faith we act on that truth.

Soul talk can never be a substitute for faith. The woman could never have talked herself into healing—not in a hundred years. But she did talk herself into seeking Jesus, and that was all she needed. And, sister, seeking Jesus is all we need too.

Soul talk is faith's companion, not its replacement. Soul talk cannot be a replacement for prayer either. Talking to your soul in exclusion of talking to your Father in heaven is never enough to bring healing to your issues. When soul talk is independent of our relationship with God, we are destined to be frustrated by our own human limitations.

Our issues can dictate our beliefs, color our actions, and affect our attitudes. *But so can our faith.* So it's essential that we center our soul talk on the truth of Scripture and on our faith in Christ. This will enable us to put positive, hopeful impressions in our thought closets.

Impressions of Truth

When I first saw (okay, I didn't literally see it, I experienced it) the movie *What About Bob?* I laughed so loudly that I actually embarrassed my husband. That's not an easy feat to accomplish because, believe me, Phil doesn't embarrass easily. Bill Murray plays a lovable but dysfunctional multiphobic named Bob Wiley. He is riddled with and debilitated by multiple issues.

The movie opens with Bob shuffling down the sidewalk on the way to his therapist's office. His pet goldfish is slung around his neck as he mutters to himself, "I feel good, I feel great…"

Immediately following his hopeful self talk, Bob collapses on the sidewalk, crushed by his issues, paralyzed by his phobias. So much for self talk. Bob Wiley demonstrates that even if self talk is positive, it is insufficient.

By the time your thirtieth birthday rolls around, your brain has been subjected to three trillion mental impressions (give or take). We need a lot more than our natural, happy, feel-good self talk to control all of those impressions. We need something supernatural. God's truth is the only valid source of worthwhile soul talk. Telling yourself *I feel good* won't make you feel good any more than telling yourself *I am skinny* will cause you to suddenly drop 30 pounds. (Bummer!) The woman with the issue of blood was bolstered because her self talk was based on truth and dependent on the trustworthiness of Christ—not herself.

So that's this first-century woman's gleaming soul-talk success story. Now, here's a glimpse of mine.

My Soul-Talk Story

My story isn't as spotlight worthy as the woman who touched Jesus and found instant healing, but even so, you might be able to relate.

During the writing of this book, I awoke one morning to a mountain of issues, and the first coherent thought I breathed into my pillow was *Ugh…I am so stressed. I am so overwhelmed, I can't even face this day…it's just too much.*

That was my self talk. And I can assure you, it didn't exactly make me want to jump out of bed. But it was true. I was stressed, overwhelmed, loaded down with too many demands, and feeling very underqualified. Ever felt like that? Who hasn't!

In that predawn fuzziness, however, when my thoughts were shadowed with worry and dread, something wonderful happened. It was as though a clarion light shot out of my thought closet to illuminate my self talk and bring clarity to the words I spoke to my soul. I began to say, *You are sufficient. You are present. You are here with me. And I can do all things through You who strengthens me!* Now, do you think I was still talking to myself when I said those things? No, my second set of pronouncements were not spoken to my soul. I was speaking to my heavenly Father.

I began the morning with self talk. I followed it with prayer and faith. And what came next?

Truthful soul talk. *I am at peace. I can press on. I can rest in God's provision. I can do this thing!*

Do you see what happened in those moments? It is super important that you do. The woman with the hemorrhage lunged forward to touch Jesus, and that is exactly what I did in my mind. In spite of all my dread, my anxieties, and the negative rubble heaped up around me, I wrenched my gaze from my own crowd of problems and focused for a moment completely on God.

And it was enough to bring healing and wellness to my soul.

Our thought closets must be filled with thoughts based on the truth of Scripture. But how in the world do we keep our thought closets orderly and under control? When our emotions are crowding in around us, how can we make sure that only productive, healthy responses stream out of our thought closets?

Spirit-Controlled Thoughts

Self-control is vital to your soul talk. But as we all know, it isn't exactly easy to maintain such relentless self-command. I've started exercise regimens and diets and made New Year's resolutions enough to prove my own lack of mastery over myself. I think I've actually broken more exercise programs and blown more diets than I've even started—which is quite a trick.

My intention is to have self-control, but the reality is that I often don't. I have learned over the years to rely instead on the *Spirit's* control in my life—God's Spirit.

Before He went to heaven, Jesus introduced His disciples to the coming Holy Spirit:

> But when the Father sends the Counselor as my representative—and by the Counselor I mean the Holy Spirit—he will teach you everything and will remind you of everything I myself have told you (John 14:26 NLT).

When we place our trust in Christ, when we have faith in Him, He gives us the gift of His Spirit to help us in this life. The Spirit fulfills several roles for us, and as we rely on Him rather than ourselves only, we are better equipped to speak healthy, truthful soul talk—and to keep the thought closet tidy!

Jesus took time to describe the Holy Spirit. He called Him a Counselor, a representative of Christ, a Teacher, and One who would remind us of truth. So what does that look like in our daily lives? How does God's Spirit help guide and control our soul talk?

The Four Roles of the Spirit

God's Spirit Counsels Us

As Phil and I prepared to celebrate our fifth wedding anniversary, we came to the conclusion that we didn't have much to celebrate. In fact, we needed counseling. We seemed stuck in an uneasy, less than perfect place in our marriage, and we couldn't get unstuck. We fought about the same things all the time, though (of course) neither of us was ever wrong. We were both convinced the problem was the other person's fault.

We loved each other even though we didn't like each other

much at that point. So with our pride pushed aside and our resolve refreshed, off to counseling we went.

After several months of hearing truth, admitting truth, and receiving truth, the result was a stronger, happier marriage between two people who not only loved each other but finally liked each other again. Larry, our counselor, was just what we needed. He was wise and objective. He listened and made us think. He was safe, and he was committed to our good, so we trusted him.

All of us get stuck on our own issues. We might know the right things to do, but we still find ourselves stalled in patterns that seem more powerful than we are. So we need a counselor.

God's Spirit is the perfect Counselor. He is safe. He is wise. He is objective. He is absolutely committed to our ultimate good. And we can trust Him never to lead us off course.

Just like Larry, God's Spirit challenges us to hear truth, admit truth, and receive truth. He counsels us through His calm, quiet voice in our spirit.

Why is His voice so quiet?

He will not shout down the noise of our busy world. He won't try to overwhelm our distractions. To hear Him, we have to quiet ourselves, step away from the frenzy, and truly *listen.*

Sometimes when we hear His gentle voice, we may mistake it for our own thoughts or intuition. But I think God's Spirit speaks to our souls more each day than we realize. He also counsels us through the words of Scripture and the remarks of others.

Listen to His voice in your spirit. Hear what He tells you as you read the pages of your Bible. And trust what He tells you.

God's Spirit Represents Christ

As a junior at Palm Beach Atlantic University, I joined an organization called the Ambassadors. These blue-blazer-clad collegiates represented our college at community events. When I signed up, I never could have imagined where it would lead me. How could I have possibly known that I would end up at the exclusive Breakers Hotel in posh Palm Beach, Florida, at an international gala...greeting none other than the Princess of Wales?

The contributing philanthropist asked our school to provide some student volunteers to help manage the guests at the gala event. So in a borrowed evening gown, I arrived with my fellow starstruck coeds. My job was to stand at the front door and welcome guests. I was instructed to ask attendees whether they were patrons or bene-factors (of course I didn't even know what that meant) and then direct them to the proper dining room.

I knew this was important because of the way our advisor coached us (okay, threatened us). We were told that our actions would directly reflect upon the university. Our duty was to represent the college well. I also figured out how big of a deal this was when security cordoned off the entryway—and the paparazzi crowded behind my partner, Jamie, and me.

The guests arrived...Bob Hope, Victor Borge, and Merv Griffin, to name a few. Then a hush fell over the lobby. There she was.

The princess.

Jamie provided colorful commentary as the much-loved royal shyly lowered her head and walked through the door to cheers and flashing cameras.

Jamie and I didn't speak as Princess Diana sauntered past in her dazzling fuchsia gown. We gawked in awe, and security whisked her to her seat. What a night.

As irresistible as the experience was, I was always mindful that I represented my university and the charity that had procured our help. Even if I wanted to scream, "Diana, I love you! Can I borrow your dress?" or though I may have wished to foxtrot with Bob Hope in his tux and tennis shoes, I would not. I was a representative of someone other than myself.

The Holy Spirit is God's representative. He mirrors God's truth. That means if you sense the Spirit leading your thoughts or guiding your actions, His guidance always lines up with the truth of God's

Word. The Spirit *never* leads us in ways that oppose Scripture. He won't; He can't. He represents and lifts up the person of Jesus. He gives illumination to the character and ways of God.

So when you believe the Spirit is guiding your life, use this test: Does this match up with the truth of the Bible? If not, send it packing to the island of misfit thoughts. We are all capable of imagination and wandering thoughts. Remember Paul's words of advice to hold those thoughts captive and see if they obey the truth of Christ. If they don't agree with Scripture, they're not from the Spirit—and they don't belong in your thought closet.

God's Spirit Is Our Teacher

I call my husband "Dr. Phil."

I do this in part because he really *is* Dr. Phil—he has his PhD. I figure after six long years of being a grad student and living on student loans, he deserves the respect.

I also think it's pretty cool that I have my very own personal Dr. Phil. (Mine isn't the famous therapist who is married to Robin McGraw with a TV show, but he does have hair!) He's a professor, so with briefcase in hand, he proclaims his motto every day as he leaves for campus.

"Going to stamp out some ignorance," he playfully announces.

That's what teachers do. They enlighten and instruct; they replace ignorance with knowledge.

God's Spirit performs that same task in our lives. He stamps out ignorance, replacing it with wisdom and discernment light-years beyond our own. He's a Mentor who teaches and guides with greater understanding than our own. Our minds need mentors.

Imagine how incredible it would be to sit with Beethoven as he instructs you in composing a symphony...or how amazing it would be to learn from Aristotle or Newton or Einstein.

When you ask God's Spirit to teach you, your mind is being mentored by none other than the God of eternity! Amazing! As a Master Teacher, He brings light wherever our understanding is dark. That means if you are relying on faulty assumptions, He will reveal the roots to you. He exposes wrong thinking and enlightens us to the truth.

Before I ever owned an audio version of the Bible, I was still able to recall much of its truth. Of course, I read it as a child and listened to countless sermons. But honestly, at that age, I was barely able to remember my own phone number. So how was I able to know and remember so much of the Scripture, even as my eyesight began to fail me?

I am convinced God's Spirit was my Teacher. My understanding of Scripture didn't come from reading commentaries or surfing seminary websites.

The Holy Spirit really does teach us. I am so grateful for this role He plays in our lives. Really, learning from Him is the only way to deal with the issues that threaten to crowd our thought closets. We need a Teacher who stamps out the ignorance that pervades our thoughts and assumptions. We need a Mentor who can offer wisdom that reaches beyond our own.

God's Spirit Reminds Us of Truth

I sat in front of a little girl and her daddy on one of my flights. We had been sitting on the tarmac for 45 minutes when the captain's voiced pierced our collective irritation. "Folks, this is your captain. We appreciate your patience. Maintenance assures me we should be ready to roll in about 15 minutes."

Fifteen minutes? At that point, it might as well have been 15 hours. Fellow passengers moaned and groaned, and I agreed. For the past 45 minutes I had been compiling a mental list of all the things I didn't like about this particular air carrier. I had been dwelling on all the bad experiences I'd had in airports lately.

We'll just see, I thought. *It'll be a miracle if this plane takes off in 15 minutes.*

But I really wasn't looking for miracles in that moment. I was pulling things out of some dark corner of my thought closet that were ugly, ill-fitting, and making me tense. Those ruminations were suddenly interrupted by the voice of the little girl in the seat behind me.

"Daddy," she said, "I spy something blue."

Determined to be cheerful, the father began to guess, "Is it that bug?" And so the game went.

"Daddy, I spy something *good*," she said.

Her dad laughed. I figured he laughed for the same reason I did at her pronouncement. It was pretty hard to spy anything good in our caged predicament.

"Is it a bag of M&Ms?" he asked.

"No," his daughter chimed.

"Is it your new shoes or your sweet smile?"

A tenderness washed over me as I eavesdropped on their exchange. Their words cut through my complaining and frustration and reminded me to fix my thoughts on "something good."

In that moment, I decided to "4:8" my thoughts as I settled back in my seat. That's Philippians 4:8 (NASB): "Finally, brethren, whatever is true, whatever is honorable, whatever is right, whatever is pure, whatever is lovely, whatever is of good repute, if there is any excellence and if anything worthy of praise, dwell on these things."

I began to let my thoughts dwell only on what was true, lovely, and of a good report. *I spy something lovely, Father,* I began to pray. *You have provided opportunities for me to experience. You have opened doors and made my path straight.* I reminded myself that delays and inconveniences were just some of the bumps along the road.

Once I began to fix my eyes on truth, I was able to enjoy the rest of my journey. When I chose to place "praiseworthy" thoughts in my thought closet, the motionless airplane became a sanctuary of peace. My issues of delays and frustration were made easier as I was able to pray and tell myself the truth.

Who is it that led me to that truth? Was it the sweet little girl and her daddy? Really, it was God's Spirit. His role is to lead us into all truth. When I was guiding my own thoughts, I was headed for a train wreck. I was quickly derailing and leading myself down a path that would further complicate my issues.

I need a better guide than my own thoughts and emotions. Do I ever! I need God's Spirit to lead me to truth. Leading myself, I don't always end up at the destination of truth.

My friend, you probably don't either. But if we follow God's Spirit, we trade our negative and unprofitable thoughts for thoughts that are positive and fruitful. He is the One who leads us to know what is worthy of our thought closet and what should be thrown in the Dumpster.

What She Said

Once upon a time, in a faraway land, there was a desperately unhappy woman who talked to herself.

Of course, she might have said any number of things. She might have told herself to cheer up, to walk on the sunny side of the street, to whistle while she worked, or to simply grin and bear it and accept her lot in life. She might even have told herself that her problems were illusions, that she was really healthy and whole.

But those aren't the sort of things she said when she spoke to her soul. What she *did* say led her to the edge of a cliff and to an act of faith more daring than anything she could have imagined since she was a little girl. When this woman talked to herself, she had an encounter that brought immediate healing of body and soul.

It was all because of what she had in her thought closet during one of the most important conversations of her life.

She told herself the truth, and that led her straight to Jesus. May you be that woman.

Soul-Talk Questions to Ponder

1. What kind of issues crowd your thought closet?

2. Are you relying on your self-control or the Spirit's control in your life?

3. Which of the four roles of the Spirit do you need most in your life?

For tips and resources to help you gain control over your thoughts, visit MeMyselfandLies.us. You'll also find a fun list of Bob Wiley multiphobic issues to make you feel better about yourself!

A SNEAK PEEK INTO KATHY TROCOLLI'S THOUGHT CLOSET

I love to be around Kathy! She's Italian, and she's got a thick New York accent! She's a Grammy nominated singer and songwriter who communicates warmth and depth in every word she sings and speaks. She's had more than her share of issues in life. Her dad died when she was only 15, and then, when Kathy was in her twenties, her mom passed away also. She's struggled through depression, bulimia, and bankruptcy. Like me, and like you, she's a woman with a few issues... but really, she is a woman with an issue of... wisdom!

"I used to think too much with my feelings. When I was bulimic for ten years, I'd feel 'you'll never get well' or 'you'll never be able to get out of this.' But God says, 'I am Healer' and 'In Me you are more than a conqueror.' Many women deal with self-esteem issues: 'I'm not good enough.' Or, 'I don't think God really forgives me.' What happens is they rely on those lies and they bring them down; but there's wisdom in the truth of God, wisdom in His promises. As I've confronted my issues and feelings with truth, I've become wiser. I'm able to take what I've learned from not being pushed by feelings but instead holding onto truth, and it's made me stronger. I hear it coming out of my mouth as wisdom. I feel like I'm wise in ways I couldn't have been before when I was drowning beneath big waves of emotion."

Part 2

SEVEN THINGS TO SAY TO YOUR SOUL

By faith I receive truth.
By faith I believe truth.
By faith I act on truth.

Thanks for staying with me. I hope you are already filling your thought closet with truth and doing some re-labeling—if you need it. We've peeked in our closets and done some rearranging, and now it's time to put some serious soul talk inside! In the coming chapters, I am going to share with you seven soul-talk phrases that have helped me. Tucking them in your closet will help you stay on the path to spiritual success.

These soul-talk statements come straight from the Old Testament, which includes four poetical books. Three of these books—Job, Psalms, and Proverbs—are also known as the "books of truth." John Calvin once called the Psalms "an anatomy of all the parts of the soul." The Psalms truly reflect each part of our souls, and that's why they speak to our deepest needs. That's also why we need to use them when we talk to ourselves.

In these final seven chapters we are going to venture through some passages from those books of truth so we can stock our thought closets with truth. Most of the soul-talk pronouncements are in the Psalms, and some are found in other books of the Bible. But one thing is for certain: Each will speak truth to your soul, and when it is applied, it will bring balance and wellness to your soul. Here is my prayer for you as you read on:

> Beloved, I pray that in all respects you may prosper and be in good health, just as your soul prospers (3 John 2 NASB).

God's truth is the light in
my thought closet.

5

TUNE IN

AWAKE, MY SOUL

My dad always told me that confession is good for the soul. Maybe…but it can also be very bad for the reputation. Even so, I'm risking my reputation with you, my readers, by letting you in on a little secret. Ready? Here goes.

I, Jennifer Rothschild, have an obsession.

There it is. It isn't pretty, but that's the reality of it.

I am obsessed with the burners on my stove, overwhelmed with the compulsion to keep them spotless and gleaming. Now that I have a gas stove, this little dysfunctional issue of mine may not require extensive therapy, but it wasn't always that way. I used to practically hover over the burners on my electric range—the burner pans, rims, and the surface beneath them were all targets of my compulsion.

Now, before you grab Dr. Phil's (the one with the TV show) latest book on obsessive-compulsive behavior, I'll tell you why I'm so fixated on clean stove burners. Until 1999, Phil and I lived in apartments or homes that never had clean cooktops. They were corroded with years of careless cooking and halfhearted cleaning. I valiantly scraped and scrubbed the old surfaces and pans, but to no avail. I even replaced the old burner pans with bright and shiny new ones, but I was never satisfied.

Why? Because I knew that underneath, down below the surface, somewhere under those gleaming burner pans, something horrible was lurking! It was the gruesome, grimy gunk produced by decades of apathy and neglect. (A little shiver runs through me even as I write these words.) I did everything I could to separate my family's food from that subterranean debris somewhere under the burners, covering my rims and pans with foil or even buying decorative burner covers to hide my shame.

Then in 1999, we moved into a 20-year-old home with a 20-year-old electric stove, and thoughts about those burners filled me with a nameless dread. (They probably hadn't been cleaned since 1979!) Nevertheless, I had a responsibility to my obsession—I mean, my family—so I marched into the kitchen and lifted the coils on the stove to inspect the burners.

When I ran my hand over the rims, the pans, and the surface beneath, I was stunned. Who would have imagined? There was actually another woman on the planet who was as obsessed with clean burners as I was! (Bless her compulsive heart.)

These were *spotless*.

Surgery could have been performed on the surface of that stove. If heaven has cooktops in its celestial dining halls, I'm convinced that this one would have been a candidate. (Actually, would it really be heaven if we had to cook and clean? I think not!)

After moving into my new home, I ended every cooking excursion by lifting the coils to wipe them clean. I removed the pans and cleaned beneath them every single time. Even when I only boiled water. I was so delighted with my clean stove, I wanted to keep it that way forever. I didn't ever want that vintage, pristine appliance to end up like the burnt and encrusted stoves of my past.

Now, I can understand that my obsession and daily cleaning routine might seem a little strange to you, but guess what—I've learned something from them. Here it is: *Keeping something clean is easier when you tend to it daily.*

The same is true with our thought closets.

When we receive new life from God, He declares that "the old life is gone. A new life has begun!"[1] Neglecting our new, clean selves allows dirt and grime to collect on the surface of our souls. It will become stuck on and hardened, it will work itself down deep, and it will certainly dull our shine. To prevent this from occurring in our lives day by day, we must be attentive.

That's where soul talk comes in. We must tell our souls to tune in.

Guarding the doors of our thought closets includes becoming alert enough to refuse any junk to enter. We want to keep our thought closets clean, and daily maintenance is the key.

How can we accomplish this? By forming the habit of reaching into our thought closets and pulling out fresh motivation to stay alert. This will keep us from living in denial or ignoring our issues.

When we wipe away the dirt from our lives by confession to God each day, we become useful, pleasant, and effective vessels. With David, then, we must tell our souls to *awake*.

Awake, My Soul

> Awake, my soul!
> Awake, harp and lyre!
> I will awaken the dawn (Psalm 57:8).

The inscription at the beginning of this psalm reads, "Of David. A miktam. When he had fled from Saul into the cave." Here's your lesson in ancient Hebrew for the day: A *miktam* was most likely a musical notation or a title for psalms of penance for sin.

Do you find it interesting that David told his soul to "awake" in the midst of a psalm about his own sin and failure? I do.

The fact is, sometimes we become sleepy and apathetic toward some of our poor choices and negative attitudes. Instead of keeping our eyes open to such things, we tend to neglect careful daily cleansing, and we grow accustomed to the grimy buildup that coats the surface of our souls. And we begin to fool ourselves into believing nothing is amiss.

The Hebrew word translated "awake" is used 65 times in the Old Testament. It means to rouse oneself, incite, or to stir up. But another way of saying it makes a lot of sense in my life: Think of it as being undeceived.

"Undeceptions" is the term C.S. Lewis used to explain milestone experiences of awareness when deception is exposed. Haze gives way to clarity, and darkness is replaced with light.

I'd call it an "aha moment." Or maybe even an "uh-oh moment," as the case may be.

Lewis noted these awakenings in many of Jane Austen's characters. He observes that in much of Austen's work, the "undeception" is the very pivot or watershed of the story." [2]

Our undeceptions are the pivots and watersheds of our personal stories too. The initial undeception that leads us to faith in God is the big one, but other, daily undeceptions keep our souls clean and thriving.

At these moments, we are most alive. We become the wise owners of our own grime and the humble recipients of God's grace. We need thought closets full of such undeceptions. We need constant reminders of truth and a heightened awareness of reality. We must constantly challenge our souls to be fully aware, awake, and tuned in. If we neglect to do so, we're in danger of forfeiting all that is most precious.

The Cost of Distraction

The morning of my twentieth wedding anniversary, I didn't awake in a five-star hotel to room service knocking on the door. No, I awakened to five loads of laundry! I rushed out of bed, threw in the first load, and woke up the boys for school! By midmorning, I had placed the wet, clean clothes in the dryer and was planning my evening out with Phil.

Later, I passed by the laundry room and noticed there was a certain *clink, clink* coming from the dryer. I assumed it was a pebble from Connor's pocket or some loose change from Clayton's.

The day went on fully stress free, and when Phil came home, he planned to change clothes for our dinner date. He needed a clean T-shirt, and I noticed he was in the laundry room a lot longer than usual. I wondered if he was folding the clothes as an anniversary gift!

He emerged with a T-shirt and a hesitant admission.

"Don't worry," he began—which meant I was immediately preparing to do just that! "I found your wedding band in the dryer."

What? I couldn't believe I had done such a thing. I was so careful with that ring! My mind rewound back to washing the dinner dishes the night before. I remembered taking the ring off. I also remembered being in a hurry and distracted by my tasks. So rather than placing it in its usual safe place, I shoved it into the pocket of my jeans.

Surely the denim protected its journey through the dryer. It came out fine, right?

When Phil didn't reply, I knew it had *not* come out fine.

"What?" I persisted. "What happened?"

Phil didn't speak. He just handed me the ring. The band was fine, but the prongs, which once held the diamond, were all bent outward, like a flower that had blossomed, petals fully open toward heaven.

"Phil…where's the diamond?"

"I couldn't find it. But don't worry, it'll be okay."

He told me he had carefully pulled out all the clothes, listened for falling stones, and felt methodically through all the fabric. I was sick. That was my treasure! It not only was the most monetarily valuable piece of jewelry I owned, it was also the most emotionally valuable. In fact, it was irreplaceable.

I lost what was most valuable to me because I was distracted by the urgency of dirty dishes! But I couldn't let it end like this, so I went into the laundry room with Phil.

"Did you check the lint cage?" I asked.

When Phil told me he hadn't, I carefully pulled it out of the dryer. As I did, I heard the tiniest little *clink* against the tile floor. It was so faint, Phil didn't even hear it. But he moved the dryer away from the wall, unscrewed the back panel, and there it was!

My diamond that Phil bought me in 1986. The diamond that cost him his life savings! The diamond I wore proudly to all my college classes that last semester. The diamond that had been on my finger when I said "I do"…when my two boys were born…when we laughed together…when I cried alone. The same diamond I wore at my brothers' weddings and grandparents' funerals. The same diamond I had worn every day of my life since 1986.

How could I have treated such a treasure with such casualness? A simple distraction could have cost me dearly.

The same happens to you and me. We risk what is most precious to us when we are not alert. Temporary distractions sidetrack us. The din and clatter or glitz and glamour of life diverts our attention from what we truly treasure. When we aren't tuned in to what is true, we are taken in by what is transient.

Anatomy of Distraction

So think about it. What do you grasp in your hand? What do you treasure most?

Now, think about the most diverting distractions you face in your life. Distractions come in many packages. Selfish indulgences distract us. So do nettlesome problems. The seemingly urgent can pull our attention away from what's really important. Only you know what truly distracts you and keeps you from prioritizing your treasures.

Let's be practical. Sometimes we don't see clearly what's going on until we spend a moment focusing.

Do you realize, my friend, how few people ever really step back from their lives and routines to gain perspective? It could very well be one of the most important things we ever do—and most of us do it so seldom. So focus with me. Take a few minutes to make a list of your top ten distractions. Just to get you rolling, I'll let you in on my list. (Or at least my top five. I don't want to overdo this confession thing.)

Distraction 1: tasks. Scouring the silverware or organizing a kitchen drawer can seem like must-do tasks at the moment, but they really aren't very urgent at all. Much as I hate to admit it, a drawer could wait a thousand years to be organized, and it really wouldn't have much effect on life, let alone eternity. Even so, this sort of task often diverts and distracts me from spending time with my family or doing something that really matters.

Distraction 2: pleasures. If I could, I would do nothing but read (or really, listen to) books. My fondest desire is to sit with a cup of coffee and a few pieces of choice dark chocolate, listening to some literary masterpiece. That defines pleasure for me, and nothing is wrong with pleasure. It's necessary for a healthy soul. But balance is also necessary.

Distraction 3: the opinions of others. What people think of me (or what I think they might be thinking of me) can cause so much internal static that I'm unable to tune in to the truth. Unless I am awake and alert, I will be too easily influenced by the opinions someone may or may not be forming about me.

Distraction 4: fear of failure. A type-A perfectionist clear through to the bone, I am constantly distracted by the desire to do things perfectly—or not do them at all. Not everything has to be done perfectly all the time. (I can't believe I'm saying this.) There is such a thing as *adequate* in some areas of life. The house doesn't need to be vacuumed every day. I appreciate having a clean kitchen floor, but that doesn't mean it has to be clean enough to serve dinner on it.

Distraction 5: disdain for conflict. Avoiding conflict with others often distracts me from approaching life in a healthy way. This distraction can keep me stuck in a pattern of relating that drains my energy and shifts my focus from thinking right thoughts.

Okay, those are the top five items on my distraction list. And in my own defense, not one single thing I've admitted to is illegal, immoral, or unethical. They are all decent and even good things. They just require balance and context.

Don't automatically assume your distractions are sinful. Only when we allow them to keep us from our treasures do they become stumbling blocks in our lives.

So what about your distraction list? What is keeping you from investing in the real treasures of your life?

What kind of treasures, you ask? Here are some of mine.

My faith. I may say I need this or that in a given period of my life, but what I truly need is a relationship with God. I treasure the intimacy I can have with Him through prayer and meditating on Scripture.

A sense of purpose. I highly value the feeling that I'm investing my life in something that has meaning, something that will last.

My family. I don't ever want to neglect my relationships with my family because of something that might seem more urgent at the time.

Self-discipline. This is a virtue I've esteemed since adolescence. Without self-command, I am subject to the whims and emotions of any circumstance. I'm like a leaf in the wind, skittering this way and that with every random gust.

God's approval. I don't want just a relationship with God; I want Him to be pleased with me. I want to sense His pleasure in the way I relate to people through the hours of the day.

So how about your treasures? Contemplate them as you look with me into another closet.

Masterpiece in a Broom Closet

When my friend Karen went to the Louvre Museum in Paris, she passed through gallery after gallery of lovely paintings. She saw scores of them, masterpiece after masterpiece, each offering an invitation to linger even while the next one beckoned.

The lengthy corridors eventually led her to a larger room that had only a few paintings at one end and even fewer along the sides. She told me how the crowd had gravitated to a lone portrait on the farthest wall. An entire wall for one painting? It would seem odd to the unacquainted, but da Vinci's *Mona Lisa* was worthy of such prominence.

That's what Scripture means when it says, "Wherever your treasure is, there your heart and thoughts will also be" (Matthew 6:21 NLT). Treasures catch our attention. Whether it's the *Mona Lisa,* the Hope Diamond, or the Crown Jewels, each piece merits a place of prominence and captures our interest.

That's true about our thoughts too. I think about what I treasure. Whenever I remove the diamond wedding band Phil gave me, I never just lay it down anywhere as I would a cup of coffee. (Okay, except for that one time!) I give it special attention and care each time I slip it from my finger.

We also put our treasures in prominent positions on the shelves of our thought closets. Those truly valuable things should have walls of their own because they are top priorities. I like to think of them as resting on the shelves just inside the door.

If you came into my bedroom and opened my closet door, the first things you would see would be the red Coach bag my sister-in-law gave me for my fortieth birthday alongside the backpack Karen brought me from her trip to Paris. Every time I open the door of the closet, my treasured bags are right there.

It's the same with our thought closets. Every time we access something from our thought closets, our treasures (our priorities) should be prominent—front and center.

But if they are so valuable, how do they sometimes get shoved to the back? That's simply the nature of distractions. They occupy more prime space than we can really afford to give them. As a result, our greatest treasures may be shoved up against the back wall, all but invisible and nearly inaccessible.

Can you imagine the custodial staff of the Louvre using the Mona Lisa Gallery as a storage room for empty boxes, extra electrical cords, and miscellaneous cleaning supplies? Can you imagine blocking the view of such a revered masterwork?

You would walk into the gallery, looking for the legendary painting. But the first thing that would assault your senses would be the strong odor of Pine-Sol. You would have to pick your way to the back wall by stepping over buckets, pushing back mop handles, and shifting boxes of supplies to make a path. And then, at the back of the room where the painting should be, a big slab of plywood is leaning against the wall! To actually get a view of da Vinci's immortal portrait, you practically have to rearrange that junky room.

That's the very thing that can happen to our thought closets unless we're awake and alert to what is happening in our lives. How then do you keep your treasures front and center?

By talking to your soul.

What you tell your soul in those crucial moments of decision throughout your day will make all the difference. When your soul is tuned in, alert and awake, your closet will remain tidy. Here's what I mean.

Whenever I'm asked to speak somewhere, I ask myself, *How does this fit into my purpose?* If I don't have a good answer, I won't accept the offer. The invitation may have been an excellent opportunity. (And believe me, when the offer involves a beach, it's awfully tempting.) But even a good thing can become a distraction if it shoves my treasures to the rear of the shelf.

When I'm asked to volunteer for something, I ask myself, *How does this impact my family?*

Here are two universal questions to ask your soul in any situation.

Does this allow me to value my treasure?
Does this cause me to treat my treasure with less value?

We need to monitor the tidiness of our thought closets. Let's keep the light on so we can clearly see what's in there.

We must tune in to our treasures and take note of what distracts us. The enemy of your soul doesn't always tempt you with obviously evil things to keep you from peace and spiritual success. No, he uses even good things to distract you from what is best.

Then, if we're not careful, distractions can slowly begin to displace our treasures. They keep our thoughts jumbled and unfocused, and we become open to deception. In fact, we can begin to forget what life is really all about.

Let me illustrate. Imagine that I started out with the worthy motive of keeping a clean and orderly house for the sake of one of my chief treasures—my family. Because I love my husband and boys, I want our home to be an attractive, peaceful place to live—a place they love coming home to.

But now imagine that I allow my legitimate desire for a clean house to gradually take over. When my oldest son walks in the front door, I scold him for not taking his shoes off. I don't allow him to sit on our best couch because I don't want to lose the showroom beauty of its cushions. I roll butcher paper down the hallway to prevent wear to our carpet.

When my youngest grabs a graham cracker, I require him to eat it over the sink lest any crumbs fall to the counter or floor.

When Phil grabs a coffee mug in the morning, I make him put it back on the shelf and use a Styrofoam cup so our pretty mugs won't be stained.

Here's where the deception enters in. Through it all, I tell myself I am prioritizing my family, my treasure. But the truth is, the treasure has been displaced—pushed to the back of the closet—by a distraction of hyperneatness.

How do we prevent that from happening? By telling our souls

to wake up, to focus on our true treasures, and to put those distractions firmly in their place.

Roaring Lion

The neighborhood where we live used to be sleepy and peaceful, and I just savored that. The street directly behind our house, lined as it was by vacant lots, was traversed mainly by squirrels and covered with a canopy of lush, towering trees.

Then everything changed. A developer sold all those lots, and construction crews moved in to build multiple dwellings. First came the grinding blades and monotonous chug of diesel bulldozers as they cleared and leveled the land. Soon these sounds were joined by the rumble of cement trucks, the whack-whack of the jackhammers, and the scream of the electric saws.

The builders began their noisy pursuits by 6:30 each morning and didn't power down until well after dinner. They continued from daylight to dusk, filling every formerly quiet moment of every day. When the new construction first began, the noisy clatter was all I could hear. And it nearly drove me crazy.

But as the summer dragged on, I noticed the clanking and banging less and less. The construction hadn't slowed down, but I had gradually become desensitized to it.

When a friend visited me, she commented about how loud it was. "Doesn't it bother you?" she asked.

"Well, it *did*," I told her. "But it's funny. I don't really notice it anymore."

Sometime later, I read a Scripture that reminded me of tuning out all that obnoxious construction noise. In 1 Peter 5:8, the great apostle compares Satan, the enemy of our souls, to a roaring lion. He says something like this: "Be careful! Be alert. Watch out. Stay awake. A roaring lion is out there, and it's stalking you and seeking to destroy you."

That passage has always confused me. How does a roaring lion sneak up on anyone? Unless you happen to be deaf, you can't help but notice his approach. His roar gives him away, even if you're busy or occupied with other things. Even a dull roar would cut through your thoughts and interrupt your senses. You don't have to be that alert to notice, do you?

That question sounds logical, but what if we heard that roar all the time? What if we heard it so often that we gradually tuned it out and became desensitized to it? It would be like living in a house next to the railroad tracks; after a while, you don't even hear the trains. We grow so accustomed to the distractions around us that we barely notice their influence.

And that's when we become easy prey.

The incessant racket of the construction used to drive me crazy, yet it eventually became commonplace. But when my friend complained about the obnoxious noise pollution, I heard it again. An *undeception* occurred, and I was awakened once again to that which I had learned to ignore.

The same is true with the roaring lion. Remember how I used to become so frustrated at myself, calling myself *idiot* all the time? Even though I had replaced that lie with the truth in my thought closet, it still pops out from time to time.

What's going on? Why does that happen?

The lion who prowls outside the door of my thought closet is making a racket with his snarled lies and growling insults. If I once agree with that hateful label of *idiot* during the day, it becomes mine. That grimy word goes right back on the shelf of the closet, and I must relabel it all over again.

Until I let that thought in, it's not my thought. It belongs to the enemy. I don't want anything he has to give, and neither do you.

Jesus said that the thief comes to kill and to steal, and that's exactly what he does. He does it one word at a time, one thought at a time. But those thoughts are not yours unless you make them yours. *I'm not good enough...I can't do anything right...I'm just going to give up...* These thoughts aren't yours until you embrace them and invite them into your thought closet. If you do, you'll find yourself wearing them again and again. But when you are alert and recognize where they come from, you will refuse them entry.

A soul that is awake is ready to do battle with the menacing, roaring lion that waits to destroy you. And just because it keeps roaring all day—just because the negative thoughts keep assaulting your mind—doesn't mean you have to become dull or desensitized.

Not if your soul is awake!

Choosing which thoughts you'll put into your closet is like shopping for clothes. You wouldn't go to the local garbage dump, pick through the refuse, and then pull out a smelly, torn, stained shirt to wear, would you? Of course not. When shopping (imagine that money is no object), you would go to Nordstrom, Saks, or Rodeo Drive and pick out only the finest, best fitting, most flattering clothes money can buy.

Why? Because you intend to wear them. The way you clothe yourself communicates your personality and your sense of personal value.

Now, transfer that picture to your thought closet. You'll clothe yourself in whatever you place in there, so shop carefully. Don't just throw something in the closet because you constantly hear it. *Loser. Idiot. Airhead. Worthless.* Refuse these thoughts entry. Those ill-fitting thoughts don't come from within you. At least not until you give them a place in your thought closet. So don't let them in.

Let the lion roar outside the door all he wants. The more consistently you refuse to embrace what he tells you, the sooner he will take his Dumpster designs elsewhere.

When I find myself stressed-out or upset with Phil, I'll often ask myself, *Who is the real enemy here? Is Phil really the one who deserves my anger?* Sometimes the enemy is stress. Sometimes the enemy is my own selfishness. But sometimes the enemy is the roaring lion.

Why fight against flesh and blood when the real enemy is invisible? Often the battle is spiritual, and we must fight that battle with spiritual weapons. "The weapons we fight with are not the weapons of the world. On the contrary, they have divine power to demolish strongholds" (2 Corinthians 10:4).

Our thought closets can become arsenals stocked with the weapons of truth. Here are some undeceptions you can use when the lion roars:

When the lion roars, "You are such a loser," say to your soul, "In all these things we are more than conquerors through him who loved us." [3]

When the lion roars, "You can't pull this off, you're too weak," say to your soul, "Do you not know? Have you not heard? The LORD is the everlasting God, the Creator of the ends of the earth. He will not grow tired or weary, and his understanding no one can fathom. He gives strength to the weary and increases the power of the weak. Even youths grow tired and weary, and young men stumble and fall; but those who hope in the LORD will renew their strength. They will soar on wings like eagles; they will run and not grow weary, they will walk and not be faint." [4]

When the lion roars, "You are abandoned. No one is on your team," say to your soul, "If God is for us, who can ever be against us? Since God did not spare even his own Son but gave him up for us all, won't God, who gave us Christ, also give us everything else?" [5]

When the lion roars, "You are alone," say to your soul, "Who shall separate us from the love of Christ? Shall trouble or hardship or persecution or famine or nakedness or danger or sword?" [6]

When the lion roars, "You've really blown it; God can't still love you," say to your soul, "For I am convinced that neither death nor life, neither angels nor demons, neither the present nor the future, nor any powers, neither height nor depth, nor anything else in all creation, will be able to separate us from the love of God that is in Christ Jesus our Lord." [7]

When the lion roars, "Nobody cares about you," say to your soul, "Praise be to the God and Father of our Lord Jesus Christ, the

Father of compassion and the God of all comfort, who comforts us in all our troubles." [8]

When the lion roars, "God doesn't really hear you when you pray," say to your soul, "The LORD is near to all who call on him, to all who call on him in truth. He fulfills the desires of those who fear him; he hears their cry and saves them." [9]

When the lion roars, "You have no value or purpose," say to your soul, "But now, this is what the LORD says...'Fear not, for I have redeemed you; I have summoned you by name; you are mine.'" [10]

When the lion roars, "This problem is unfixable," say to your soul, "O Sovereign LORD! You have made the heavens and earth by your great power. Nothing is too hard for you!" [11]

When the lion roars, "You really should panic," say to your soul, "Don't worry about anything; instead, pray about everything. Tell God what you need, and thank him for all he has done. If you do this, you will experience God's peace, which is far more wonderful than the human mind can understand. His peace will guard your hearts and minds as you live in Christ Jesus." [12]

When the lion roars, "You can't count on anything or anyone," say to your soul, "Do not let your hearts be troubled. Trust in God; trust also in me. In my Father's house are many rooms; if it were not so, I would have told you. I am going there to prepare a place for you. And if I go and prepare a place for you, I will come back and take you to be with me that you also may be where I am." [13]

When the lion roars, "You will never find peace," say to your soul, "Peace I leave with you; my peace I give you. I do not give to you as the world gives. Do not let your hearts be troubled and do not be afraid." [14]

When the lion roars, "You have no willpower," say to your soul, "For God did not give us a spirit of timidity, but a spirit of power, of love and of self-discipline." [15]

So be aware of the real enemy. Talk to yourself about his tactics, and tell your soul to tune in. Remind your soul that the One who lives within you is greater than the one who roars at the door!

If you have to be compulsive about something, be obsessed with the desire to guard your treasures and speak truth to your soul.

Soul-Talk Questions to Ponder

1. What undeception has brought you liberty?

2. Have you identified your real enemy?

3. Do you need to tell your soul to tune in more often?

For tips and resources to keep you tuned in, visit MeMyselfandLies.us. You'll also find help for keeping a clean soul—and oven.

Passages to Ponder

Be of sober spirit, be on the alert. Your adversary, the devil, prowls around like a roaring lion, seeking someone to devour (1 Peter 5:8 NASB).

With all prayer and petition pray at all times in the Spirit, and with this in view, be on the alert with all perseverance and petition for all the saints (Ephesians 6:18 NASB).

Keep watching and praying that you may not enter into temptation; the spirit is willing, but the flesh is weak (Matthew 26:41 NASB).

In addition to all this, take up the shield of faith, with which you can extinguish all the flaming arrows of the evil one (Ephesians 6:16).

A SNEAK PEEK INTO LIZ CURTIS HIGGS'S THOUGHT CLOSET

Being with Liz is like reuniting with an old friend who makes you feel safe and special—even if it's the first time you've met!

She speaks at Christian women's conferences all around the globe, and she's written more than 35 books, including her bestseller, *Bad Girls of the Bible*. So, I asked the original "bad girl" how she keeps her soul alert to the bad thoughts that so easily bombard all of us…

"Two verses, memorized in my early days as a believer, help me stay on track on a daily, hourly, even by-the-minute basis. One verse is short and to the point: 'Pray without ceasing' (1 Thessalonians 5:17). My conversations with the Lord aren't just at mealtime or bedtime or crunch time. I talk to Him constantly. Often in my thoughts, and many times with my lips, I call out to Him, 'Forgive me, Lord. I know better than to let my mind wander there.'

"The other verse is: 'We are destroying speculations and every lofty thing raised up against the knowledge of God, and we are taking every thought captive to the obedience of Christ' (2 Corinthians 10:5). Every time my Bad Girl thoughts show up, I mentally snatch them out of the air and hand them over to Jesus—the sooner, the better, before they find a cozy spot to take root.

"I spent so many years mired in the muck of living for self, hanging out with the Enemy, that when Christ came into my life at age 27, I saw the dramatic difference between Satan's lies and God's truth. That childlike understanding has stuck with me.

"So, when someone or something is bent on hurting me—stirring up feelings of jealousy or envy, inadequacy or inferiority, hopelessness or uselessness—I recognize the destructive power behind those feelings. They are never of God. They are always of the Enemy.

"The only way to get rid of that bad boy is to send him packing. I tell him to go home in no uncertain terms. 'Go to _____.' Right. That place. I remind him that he is a loser, and Christ is the victor. That I belong, body and soul, to Almighty God. Every time, without fail, he withdraws from the battle, and my feelings and thoughts quickly lighten."

I will not think with my feelings.

6

LOOK UP

HOPE IN GOD, MY SOUL

Whoever coined the phrase "fraidy cat" has never met my oversized orange tabby.

Justice weighs about 15 pounds and looks like the feline equivalent of Rocky Balboa. He has patches of hair missing and squinty eyes bordered by a fat, furry face, slightly swollen from one too many boxing matches with the neighborhood cats. And as you can imagine, he has an attitude to match.

One of his favorite things to do is spread his massive girth across the top of the stairs that lead down to our basement. I, on the other hand, strongly object to his choice of a resting place.

On that very top stair, the battle of wills between Justice and Jennifer began. I took the first step down toward the basement one morning, but something smushy made me lose my balance. Before I could tell what it was, a disinterested *mew* rose from beneath my feet.

"Justice!" I squealed. "Get out of the way!"

My protests and yelling, however, did not move him at all. He had staked out his spot, and he didn't intend to move. I continued downward, assuming that the footprint on his back would have motivated him to move his furry physique.

Hours later, I climbed back up the stairs while on the phone with my friend Karen. I stopped midsentence with a yelp. I stumbled, dropped the phone, and arrived not so gracefully on the main floor.

I could hear Karen calling from the receiver, "What happened? Are you okay?"

Then I heard it. *Mew.*

This time, he sounded a little more interested and a lot more irritated. So was I. I screamed louder at the cat. "Justice, MOVE!"

I brushed myself off, found the phone, and reassured Karen that I was still alive and whole and that a cat named Justice would no longer sprawl himself on the top stair. After all, I must have scared at least one of his nine lives right out of him.

Still later, I headed back downstairs to get my laptop. I'm sure you've guessed it. There sat Justice. This time, I caught myself and managed enough balance (if you're a cat lover you should skip this next part) to kick that cat on his well-padded heinie.

He still didn't move.

This little beast should be the mascot for all the No Fear paraphernalia. He was utterly unshakable.

Later in the day, when my indignation had subsided, I had to laugh about it. *Justice the Immovable!* You've heard of *The Cat in the Hat?* This was The Cat in Cement.

I wonder why we aren't more like that? Unshakable and fearless. Undaunted by the bumps and bruises and shouts that come across our path. Instead, we fall into despair. We run like fraidy cats when life kicks rudely against our ribs.

It doesn't have to be that way! We too can be unshakable when we tell our souls to look up and make hope our anchor.

Grab the Anchor

The Princess and the Goblin by George MacDonald was one of J.R.R. Tolkien's favorite stories. It's one of mine too. At one point in the tale, the young Princess Irene lets fear overcome her and foolishly chooses to run from the safety of her castle out into the dark mountains.

In his prose, MacDonald muses, "But that is the way fear serves us: it always sides with the thing we are afraid of."

That's why we can't ever side with fear, because fear is never on our side. And we can't let fear and despair shake and intimidate us.

Fear betrays; hope never does. Fear and despair make us quiver; hope makes us unshakable.

Rather than giving in to fear or despair, we tell our souls to hope. Hope will always be on your side, cheering you on and defending you. Despair always works against you. It serves what you most want to avoid. It deceives, manipulates, and eventually overcomes.

Hope anchors us because it provides spiritual grounding. Hope brings stability to every part of our being: physical, mental, emotional, and spiritual. It's something steady to hold onto when fear and despair rock our world. We speak the language of hope when we tell our souls to look up.

What the Psalmist Said to His Soul

We all face shaky times. And we all have felt the tug toward despair, like a strong undertow in treacherous surf. Life presents plenty of opportunities for our souls to be downcast.

Downcast isn't a word we use very often, but we use similar words all the time: *sad, disappointed, bummed out, bluesin'...*

We want to be firmly grounded and unshakable, but sometimes we just can't seem to shake the blues. The earth itself seems to tip us toward anxiety and despair.

Ever since God foreclosed on the Garden of Eden and sent Adam and Eve packing into the wilds, despair has been part of the human condition. Going back just a few millennia, we can read a startling example of deep despair meeting up with soul talk in a head-to-head battle. And soul talk won.

In the book of Psalms, an unidentified psalmist opens his personal journal and allows us to look down on the tearstained pages. In verse 5 of Psalm 42, he writes these words:

> Why are you downcast, O my soul?
> Why so disturbed within me?

The first hundred or so times I read that, I thought the psalmist was reprimanding or scolding his soul. *Now, come on, soul...you know better. Act like a believer! You're not supposed to be depressed or downcast. What's wrong with you? You're supposed to have hope. Better buck up, soul.*

But just lately, I've seen something more than scolding in that internal dialogue. After all, everyone feels depressed at times. Even normally happy people get the blues. Christians who have every reason to hope experience feelings of hopelessness. We wish for things to be one way, but our wishes rarely match the way things are. Losing hope is easy and even natural sometimes.

So the more I thought about it, I began to better understand what the writer of this psalm was saying. I think he was doing some honest soul exploration. His mind searched his soul for the reason behind his feelings. So he interviewed his soul. And he began with a simple question.

Why? "Why are you downcast?"

The psalmist surveyed the contents of his thought closet to find out why everything hanging in there was in shades of blue. I've been impressed with two things about this man's interview.

First, I like his inquiry because it's honest. He acknowledges that he feels despair. Believe it or not, that's a positive first step on the path out of the pit. Despair won't go away just because we ignore it, run from it, drown it out, or deny it. A soul in despair must be honest enough to admit the truth. That's where it all begins.

Second, I also like the writer's question because it's perceptive. He asks his soul why because he recognizes that there is a cause for feeling downcast. Something is amiss. He knows his soul is out of sorts and that it didn't just get that way for no reason. So he decides to trace the source by scrutinizing his thought closet.

> Why are you down in the dumps, dear soul?
> Why are you crying the blues? (Psalm 42:5 MSG)

Have you ever asked your soul questions like that? *Why are you in despair? Why so down, so negative, so anxious?* If you've never done that, now would be a good time to start. Grab a cup of coffee, take a seat at your kitchen table, and have an interview with your soul.

Table Talk

I hope you really do sit down at a table. Your table is good for quite a number of things. You can eat at it, work at it, or pile things on top of it. You might even use it as an impromptu stepladder when you're in a pinch. Or you can join me and use your table as an illustration, a way to start your soul interview.

Imagine with me for a minute that you *are* a table. (Now, work with me here, okay?) What kind of table? It really doesn't matter. You can be a card table from Walmart or a polished piece of cherrywood from Ethan Allen. Just make sure you have four legs. Why? Because if even one leg is loose or damaged, the whole table will be shaky and imbalanced, unable to perform its appointed tasks. All four legs are needed to keep the table in balance.

The same is true with you and me. When one of the essential areas of our lives is loose, damaged, neglected, or removed, we will be shaky and imbalanced. We will easily tip and fall into despair. A damaged table can't possibly bear any extra weight, so when the stress and the load piles up, we wobble, lean, or just collapse. We need four essential supports in order to keep an even keel.

Your Emotional Leg

"Life is a train of moods like a string of beads," wrote Emerson, "and as we pass through them they prove to be many-colored lenses, which paint the world their own hue, and each shows us only what lies in its own focus."

That's a poet's way of saying that emotions are precious and powerful, but they have their limitations. If you try to think with your feelings, for instance, you fall into all manner of false conclusions. When our minds take flight and our emotions take over, we get shaky. So shaky we might collapse or fall into despair.

Emotions are supposed to serve and strengthen us. Left to themselves, however, they enslave and deplete us. We need a thought closet well stocked with timeless truth, or we will clothe ourselves with the feelings of the moment.

As a teenager, I was prone to moodiness. (I'm sure you never were.) Once when my train of moods grew especially dark, my dad told me a story from his college days, hoping to snap me back into reality. One of the guys in his dorm, it seems, had fallen victim to a college prank. While he slept, his "friends" smeared his upper lip with limburger cheese. Awaking from his nap and realizing it was time for class, the young man grabbed his books and hurried out the door with the other guys.

On the way, he wrinkled up his nose and said, "It stinks out here." When the entourage passed a trash can, he proclaimed, "That garbage is *really* rancid." Entering the classroom, he asserted, "This room reeks!"

The obvious application is that his problem was right under his own nose. That was pretty much true when I was grumpy, sad, or angry.

Our problems usually have less to do with our circumstances than with the way we choose to *feel* about them. All too often, the problem isn't out there, it's right under our noses. The emotional leg of the table gets shaky when it tries to bear the weight alone—as if it were the only leg designed to deal with the issues of life. Overworked and under too much pressure (especially in tables with lots of estrogen), the leg ends up making the whole table unstable.

Remember, feelings aren't always the same things as facts.

They might feel real, but that doesn't mean they always correspond with reality. Of course, I'm not suggesting we throw our feelings out and discount them. No way. Emotions are valid and important gifts from God. But because they can be very powerful and very present, we can easily believe they represent facts. When that happens, take a moment to have a little interview with your soul.

Ask your soul why you feel the way you do, just as the psalmist did.

Go ahead. Your soul can handle it. In fact, your soul *needs* to think it through. The question acknowledges that your emotions are real and that they matter, but that they might not be based on facts. It will also guide you—like an intuitive detective—toward discovering the real source of your feelings.

You can also ask your soul, *Do I think with my feelings? Do my feelings serve me well, or am I their slave?*

Questioning your soul allows you to honestly assess your emotions so you can calibrate them with truth—and tighten up that shaky leg.

Your Physical Leg

We are fearfully and wonderfully made, so we need to be wise stewards of our bodies. Never discount the impact of physical wellness on our souls' wellness. Feelings of despair might really be our bodies' signal that we need to meet some basic needs. Your body needs adequate rest, healthy food, and moderate exercise.

Being rested sure makes a difference in the way we look at life. We all know this is true for toddlers and teenagers, but it's also true in any decade of life you find yourself in.

You know what happens when you are tired. You're prone to cry easier, lose your temper faster, forget things sooner, drop things more often, and experience the fog of fatigue settling over your brain. I'm saying "you," but really, that's my autobiography! If the physical leg of your table gets too weak and tired, the whole table feels shaky. So before you assume the worst about your situation, make sure you've had enough rest. You might simply be exhausted.

The food we choose to eat matters too. You can memorize the food pyramid and count calories if you'd like, but poor eating habits are not usually due to a lack of knowledge. We eat poorly due to lack of discipline and desire. (I know that hurts.)

I'm trying to keep my hands out of a stash of chocolate while I type this! The sad list goes on and on...too much sugar, not enough water, too many bad carbs, not enough fruits and veggies. Yeah, yeah, yeah. My friend, we know what it takes. We just need for it to take!

We can't afford to discount the unseen impact this has on our balance and stability.

I've tried everything over the years to figure this food thing out! And for me, I've found that the way I deal with this best is to eat often. I try to keep my portions small, the size of the palm of my hand. I don't drink my calories; I eat them. That means I do the eight glasses of water a day (which keeps the dark chocolate option always open). You know what works for you, and if you don't, figure it out—you're worth it, sister! You need your body to serve you because you've got a lot of life to enjoy!

And lastly, to be attentive to your physical needs, you can't neglect exercise. Well, actually, I am living proof that you *can* neglect exercise. A better way to phrase that is to say we shouldn't neglect exercise.

Researchers have found that when we exercise, our pituitary glands can release as much as five times as many mood-boosting beta-endorphins as they do when we are resting. It's true. I always enjoy such a nice feeling of wellness when I get off the treadmill. I just wish I felt that way before I got on. I would be much more motivated!

An Arabian proverb says, "He who has health has hope, and he who has hope has everything." So exercise some discipline to move more. I do it by associating something I love with something I don't love—books with exercise. I am a book fanatic, and I listen to my favorite books only when I am on the treadmill. That really motivates me to get on board!

If you interview your soul and answer honestly, you can discern if this leg is giving you the support you need to be unshakable. So take a brisk walk, drink a glass of water, grab a carrot stick, lay down for a spell, and think about it.

Mark Twain said, "The only way to keep your health is to eat what you don't want, drink what you don't like, and do what you'd rather not." I'm learning that discipline is doing what I don't want to do so I can do what I want to do. Are you being good to your body? How can you strengthen this leg?

Your Mental Leg

You have a power plant right between your ears. It's called your brain. I hope you realize how capable you are of thinking, learning, and growing in understanding. Even more than that, I hope you realize that this isn't just a capacity you have. It's one of your most basic needs.

Brains like to be challenged. Your mind needs to have something to do, or it will *create* something to do—something that might not be so constructive. This leg needs to dance. Your body needs exercise, and so does your brain. Polish writer Stanislaw J. Lec agrees: "You have to climb to reach a deep thought." And all of that climbing is sure to make you stronger.

If you don't fully strengthen your brain, it will wiggle and jiggle itself just to alleviate the dullness and find a channel for all of its energy.

Oh, girl, I was bored for years and didn't even know it. My mind had nowhere useful to go, so I spent too much time contemplating the lesser things of my life. I was left with a "poor me" attitude, a martyr complex, and bouts of depression. With way too much idle mental time, I overanalyzed my marriage and husband. The results were unreasonable expectations, despair, and frustration.

When I finally asked my soul why it felt the way it did, I began to trace some revealing patterns. I got a clue that I might need something bigger and better to think about. That's when I broke out of my mental lethargy and subscribed to the Talking Books Library. I began listening to volumes of books on all sorts of subjects...histories, biographies, and classics, both fiction and nonfiction. A whole new world opened to me. New thoughts brought fresh stimulation, and my whole perspective on life began to open up like a flower in the sunlight.

The places I hoped to travel to, I visited through the vehicle of the written word. Pictures I always wanted to see were projected on the screen of my mind in vivid color by means of the artful expressions of authors like James and Hawthorne.

My mind grappled with mysteries and stretched to view exotic landscapes—local, foreign, and even alien! I was learning, and for the first time in my life, I realized I had been bored for decades and never really knew it. Without interviewing my soul, I would have never come to that liberating conclusion. Maria Mitchell wrote, "We have a hunger of the mind which asks for knowledge of all around us, and the more we gain, the more is our desire; the more we see, the more we are capable of seeing."

Ask your soul to examine that leg, so frequently the most neglected leg. See if it is being adequately challenged. If not, you can take some simple steps to make the necessary repairs. Spend a few minutes each day reading something that interests and challenges you. Then ponder it during the day. Pick up a journal and record your thoughts and questions. Join a book club or audit a class from your local university. Feed your curiosity, and you'll stimulate an enjoyable, insatiable hunger.

Your Spiritual Leg

Hopelessness, fear, and depression often grow out of unsatisfied longings. C.S. Lewis said, "If I find in myself a desire which no experience in this world can satisfy, the most probable explanation is that I was made for another world."

A deep longing resides in each of us that only God can meet. Neglecting this longing doesn't make it go away. It will only continue to grow, and left untended, it leads to a sort of melancholy of the soul. You begin to feel homesick for places you have never been!

We can try to fill the longing with relationships, religion, volunteerism, or just being good. But the deep ache from the bottom of our souls can only be satisfied in a relationship with God. Intimacy with the One who shaped your heart will truly and deeply satisfy your soul.

When the spiritual leg of your table isn't secure, the weakness isn't always obvious. This seems to be the invisible leg, but it is really the weight-bearing leg of the table. When it's off-kilter, the symptom shows up in the other three legs. When our spiritual needs aren't met, we experience the effects physically, emotionally, and mentally. When this one leg wobbles, the whole table trembles.

Your spiritual nature is the part of you that is eternal. It's the part of you that will live forever and longs to deeply connect with your heavenly Father.

The thing is, we are finite beings, and we can't reach the infinite God on our own. So, He came to us so we could know Him and be with Him forever. Jesus clothed His deity in our humanity so the deepest longing of our souls could be met. As we transfer trust from ourselves to Him, we find deep satisfaction, and our longing is fulfilled.

Have you had that longing met? Until you do, you will have a shaky table. Turn to appendix 2 to see how your spiritual longings can be met once and for all.

Asking why helps you to take steps to tighten up the table legs. So pull out the repair kit and get to work on your legs. You are way too valuable to live with wobbly hope. You'll soon find yourself walking on the road to stability and speaking hope to your soul.

Hope in God

Telling a hungry person to be filled and then walking away just doesn't cut it. You're not going to fill a starving man and satisfy his hunger with mere words.

The same is true with hope. Telling yourself to hope won't lift you on wings of anticipation, inspire you to author a book on the power of optimism, or land you on TV lauding how hope changed your life. Despair is heavier than that, and all the talk in the world won't lighten the load.

Sometimes you just don't have a leg to stand on. You may be physically spent, emotionally raw, mentally bored, or spiritually empty. Deal with those issues first. They will become the rope that is fixed to the anchor of hope. Once those essentials are strong enough to carry the load of life, you'll be ready to speak hope to your soul.

Hope is a choice. It might have feelings that accompany it, but hope is not a feeling. It's more. It's certain. It's a decision that allows us to be steady and sure. It anchors us to something greater than ourselves and has great influence over how you feel when things get difficult.

When you are confronted with a circumstance that challenges you, you have two choices. You can say to your soul, *Soul, you might as well get depressed, fall into despair, and lose heart.* Or you can say to your soul, *Soul, you might as well have hope, believe in something good happening, and place your expectation in the goodness of God.*

That's what the psalmist did. He attached his hope in God to a promise from God. He asked, "Why are you in despair, O my soul? And why have you become disturbed within me?" Then he told his soul, "Hope in God, for I shall again praise Him for the help of His presence" (Psalm 42:5 NASB).

He reminded his soul that the help of God's presence was a guarantee. And that left him with no reason to lose hope. The promise is for you too, my friend.

A second time, he tells his soul to hope in God. This time, he reminds his soul of another guarantee: "I shall yet praise Him, the help of my countenance and my God" (verse 11). God will be the help of your countenance also, my friend, and sometimes our countenances need the help. Do you realize the impact a true, sunny, from-the-heart smile can have on those around you—and on you yourself? Sometimes, smiling is like pulling open the blinds and letting the morning sunlight stream in.

What have you said to your soul lately? When you are confronted with a catastrophe, a disappointment, or a bad situation, avoid the self-sabotage of eating a gallon of ice cream at midnight and sleeping till noon the next day. That's just another way to speak despair to your soul!

Do something different. Sit down for your soul interview and check out your four legs. And then tell your soul to choose hope.

Is it really as simple as a choice? Oh, my friend, it's as *difficult* as a choice. But why choose despair when you can choose hope? To not choose hope is to choose despair by default.

Even if telling yourself to hope doesn't immediately result in a swell of optimism that lifts your spirit, it will serve to shift your focus. Hope makes you focus on the potential of something broader, someone bigger, and somewhere better. That's what you see when your soul looks up.

What You See When You Look Up

Something Broader

Phil and I took a seat outside a local coffee shop where he opened the newspaper and started to read aloud. I love it when we get to do this, but this time it brought tears.

The article he read was about a young woman named Minda Cox. She was born in India 18 years ago without arms or legs. After learning about her, her soon-to-be American mom began to secure her adoption. It took longer than planned because Minda didn't even have a fingerprint for her legal papers or passport. Phil read slowly as we both choked up with emotion.

Then with surprise and delight we read on and learned that Minda is a budding artist. She cradles a brush between her chin and shoulder and paints with such talent and skill that her art is worthy of its own showing. Her artistry is impressive, but what really inspired me was a list her mom found in her backpack when she was in fourth grade. It contained 127 things she would do if she had arms or legs.

She would set her own alarm clock. Make the sign of the cross. Walk where there aren't sidewalks. Jump with joy and clap her hands. She'd be tall.

Minda's list helped me broaden my view. I may not be able to see, but I can use my arms and hands to set my own alarm clock and hug my kids. I may be in physical darkness, but I can walk where there aren't sidewalks, kneel in prayer, and jump for joy. I have losses for sure. But I also have many gains. And so do you. When we look up, we broaden our view and are able to see that our losses remind us of all that we have received.

Hope is lost when we focus only on our own problems. But choosing hope widens our perspective. Epictetus acknowledged, "People are not disturbed by things, but by the view they take of them." You will see the true size and shape of your problem more clearly when you look at it from a different angle.

Difficulties can look awfully big, and they will try to stare you down and force you to despair. But you don't have to let them.

So let your adversity become your friend. Ask of it, *What can you teach me about my strengths? What can I learn from you about my weakness? How can this problem strengthen me? What have I gained because of this problem?*

Helen Keller's eyes never saw what I still remember seeing as a girl. Her ears never heard the sound of children playing or the music of the great classical composers. She lived her 88 years without a single sound or sight to enjoy, yet she became a woman with an incredibly broad view. So she could say with great conviction, "The most pathetic person in the world is someone who has sight but has no vision."

So put hope to work, my friend, and look around. Look up. You'll discover that there's much more to life than the cloud that hangs over your head.

Someone Bigger

The most hopeful people I know are those who place their trust in God. Liberated from the need to always be in control, they are able to rest in Him rather than struggle to avoid difficulties in this life. They don't become hopeless because their hope is in God, not in themselves or their circumstances changing. I have hope even in blindness because I'm learning to focus on the goodness of God.

It's not a once-and-forever choice. It's a choice I make day by day.

God is bigger than your problem and bigger than your perception of your problem. I love the words God spoke to tiny Judah at a time when their enemies were great, their future was uncertain, and their faith was in tatters:

> Was my arm too short to ransom you?
> Do I lack the strength to rescue you?...
> Surely the arm of the LORD is not too short to save,
> nor his ear too dull to hear. [1]

Your difficulties may seem higher than you can see, deeper than you can tunnel beneath, and wider than you can walk around. Nevertheless, the arm of the Lord is never too short to grip you by the hand and take you over, under, around, or through any difficulty that life brings to your doorstep.

By the way, your soul needs to hear words like those. Tell your soul to hope in God (Psalm 42:11), and you will be infused with strength beyond your circumstance.

Somewhere Better

At a Dallas book signing, a tearful woman handed me her book. When I asked her name, she replied, "Jeannie, but I must tell you about my husband, Bruce."

She recounted his story, telling me how he had been severely wounded by a gunshot as a young man. As a result, he was a quadriplegic. Jeannie, however, spoke with such admiration of her husband's strength and unshakable hope. She told me that over the years, Bruce had heard many kind and empathetic remarks, such as "I bet you can't wait to get to heaven so you can walk."

Bruce's response to such remarks reveals what he had stored away in his thought closet. "I'm not so interested in getting to heaven so I can walk or run or jump," he replies. "I long for heaven because there I can kneel."

Hope always seems to involve waiting, longing. Waiting is often depleting and longing can be dissatisfying. It's all a matter of where we put our hope. If our hope is in right circumstances, life will always feel wrong, for it has more than its fair share of disappointments and struggles. But when hope is grounded in someplace better than here, our view of this life diminishes.

Bruce wasn't fatigued because his hope wasn't in his healing. He was fortified because his hope was somewhere better.

What if, like Bruce, your greatest hope was to kneel in heaven someday? You would be strengthened and never disappointed because your ultimate hope would be in a reality beyond the shifting, drifting situations of this uncertain life. I want that, don't you? That kind of hope enables you to walk by faith, run with endurance, and soar above your circumstances.

"Hope," says the old Irish proverb, "is the physician of each misery." Oh, may our longing to kneel always be greater than our longing to be healed. My friend, never choose despair when you can choose hope. Despair will never bolster you, support you, or encourage you. It will begin your slow demise.

Despair and fear throw you into a tailspin and land you in the arms of your enemy. But hope, though invisible, will never leave you, will always hearten you, and will be the best medicine for your soul. Hope says, "He who limps is still walking." [2]

So think about the best. Don't focus on the worst. As Helen Keller said, "We could never learn to be brave and patient if there were only joy in the world."

Hope whispers when the world shouts. It sits with you when you are alone. It is a blanket of comfort when you are afraid. It is the warmth that burns with the flame of truth. It is the foundation upon which your life can rest securely.

Hope will ground you, anchor you, and make you unshakable. And by the way, your thought closet always has room for a little more hope and a lot less despair!

Soul-Talk Questions to Ponder

1. Which leg or legs do you need to tighten?

2. Do you think with your feelings?

3. Where is your hope?

4. What promises from God do you need to remind your soul of to help you not lose hope?

For some tips and resources to keep you looking up, visit MeMyselfandLies.us. You'll also find a list of my favorite books to keep you from mental boredom, an interesting interview about optimism with Dr. Elizabeth Rozell, and more about Minda Cox.

Passages to Ponder

This hope we have as an anchor of the soul, a hope both sure and steadfast (Hebrews 6:19 NASB).

Be joyful in hope, patient in affliction, faithful in prayer (Romans 12:12).

I pray also that the eyes of your heart may be enlightened in order that you may know the hope to which he has called you (Ephesians 1:18).

> But those who hope in the LORD
> will renew their strength.
> They will soar on wings like eagles;
> they will run and not grow weary,
> they will walk and not be faint (Isaiah 40:31).

"For I know the plans that I have for you," declares the LORD, "plans for welfare and not for calamity to give you a future and a hope" (Jeremiah 29:11 NASB).

Therefore we do not lose heart, but though our outer man is decaying, yet our inner man is being renewed day by day. For momentary, light affliction is producing for us an eternal weight of glory far beyond all comparison, while we look not at the things which are seen, but at the things which are not seen; for the things which are seen are temporal, but the things which are not seen are eternal (2 Corinthians 4:16-18 NASB).

A SNEAK PEEK INTO CHONDA PIERCE'S THOUGHT CLOSET

Chonda is a much-loved comedian and author. In fact, she currently holds the record for the most Gold and Platinum DVD certifications of any female comic in history. She does make me laugh every time I'm with her, but all that humor comes from some places in her life that just aren't that funny. Through those hard places, though, she has learned to talk to herself, and it's made all the difference. She gave me a sneak peek into her thought closet. To sort fact and feeling, she makes a list of lies and truths when she talks to herself. It's helped her speak truth and hope to her soul. And when I tried it, it helped me too. I bet it'll be a big help to you also!

"I've had to learn to rehearse in the dark what I have learned in the light. Hopelessness needs to be on the list of lies, because our feelings lie to us, especially women. I always say that if Satan is the author of lies then depression is his cell phone because depression is based on feeling hopeless. But...hope is Christ. Colossians says 'I'm going to give you a secret that has been kept hidden from generations but is now disclosed to the saints.' In other words, when Jesus came the secret was out. 'And the secret or mystery is this...Christ in you, the hope of glory' (Colossians 1:26-27 paraphrased)."

*I can't always change my circumstances,
but I can change my reaction to them.*

7

CALM DOWN:

I HAVE STILLED AND QUIETED MY SOUL

A wise philosopher named Phyllis Diller once said, "Never go to bed mad. Stay up and fight!"

As much as I hate to admit it, I have at times been quick to follow such not-so-wise advice.

Phil and I lived in Tallahassee while he was completing his PhD. We had a little money, a little time, and a little boy. All in all, it was really a happy season of life—with one little exception.

Actually, it wasn't so little. I was overwhelmed with stress and couldn't figure out how to manage it. Ever felt like that?

I internalized everything. My weak survival skills showed up in things like constant illness and chronic aggravation. Rage simmered just below the surface of my placid demeanor.

One afternoon, Phil called from campus. I don't even remember what he said or what he wanted, but I certainly remember my response. I remember raising my voice. Okay, I was really yelling.

I also remember hanging up the phone.

Well, I actually remember slamming it down while he was mid-sentence. I felt like a volcano must feel right before it erupts—hot, quivering, and rumbling from the roots. I was furious. My internalizing days were officially over.

With one completely abandoned and reckless move, I external-ized in a big way. I swung my leg back and then forward, kicking the wall as hard as I could. The pictures shook, and that made me feel some satisfaction. The things on the shelf all wobbled in mortal fear of my wrath. That made me feel like I was proving my point. Then the wall crackled. I heard drywall falling and splintering off. I felt my foot woefully wedged within the wall while dust blew into my face.

I was stuck.

When I pulled my tennis shoe out, the hole only got bigger. I didn't feel so good. I had damaged our rented apartment, and really, I had no excuse.

I had heard of the "count to ten" anger management rule. But I didn't want to count; I wanted to explode. I had given full control to my anger, and it wasn't a pretty sight.

I'm only five-two, so my kick didn't land very high on the wall—not nearly high enough to cover the hole with a picture. So racked with guilt and remorse, I got a piece of paper from the desk, wrote "Love covers a multitude of sins," and taped it over the hole!

Ralph Waldo Emerson said, "Coolness and absence of heat and haste indicate fine qualities."

I guess that means the opposite is also true. Red hot rage and volcano-like eruptions indicate not so fine qualities. Our reactions reveal the temperature inside our thought closets. We can use soul talk to keep the thermostat at a cool and steady temperature. We must learn to still and quiet our souls, to tell our souls to calm down.

Speaking Shalom to Your Soul

The Old Testament word for *peace* is based on the Hebrew greeting *shalom*. This peaceful-sounding word is really a prayer that asks God to secure a person's well-being. You can still and quiet your soul by speaking *shalom* to yourself. It's like inviting wellness to your soul—to your thought closet. Peace like this brings life's highest and best benefits. And take it from one who knows—it's much better than exploding to no one's benefit.

Experiencing real *shalom* seems nearly impossible in our chaotic lives, though. Peace, calm, and tranquility seem just beyond our grasp. And let's face it, we all have times of stress, feel overwhelmed, and have telephone conversations that are...well, less than peaceful. But peace is a quality that can characterize our inner world even while our outer world goes crazy.

Poets and philosophers have pondered the source of peace for centuries. Jesus reveals its source with great clarity: "Peace I leave with you; my peace I give you. I do not give to you as the world gives" (John 14:27).

Before we can really appreciate the source of peace, we need to acknowledge why we have angry, smoldering embers in our thought closets to begin with. We must identify the source of our anger.

Loosen the Grip

Do you realize how difficult it is to be a blind control freak?

By nature, I am a planner. I strategize, organize, analyze, and then watch as everything falls into perfect place.

But add blindness to that equation. I can assure you that what was once pretty difficult is now practically impossible.

A long time ago, I had to reconcile myself to the fact that I wasn't in control and really could never be in control as I wished to be. The real reconciliation wasn't with the disappointment that blindness had taken away my control. It was with the realization that ultimate control was never mine to begin with.

Did you catch that? Blindness didn't take away my control. It simply exposed that I never had ultimate control in the first place! And, my friend, neither do you. If we truly had control over all the events of our lives, we would have chosen when we were born, to whom we were born, and where we were born. We would have selected our own names and even our own DNA. And I can guarantee you that I would have chosen DNA that made me as tall as Julia Roberts rather than as short as Jennifer Rothschild!

So much of the anger in our lives comes from unmet expectations and frustration that we don't have ultimate control.

Blindness has forced me to come to terms with this and has compelled me to loosen my grip on the illusion of control—finger by finger, day by day.

Control over the events of our lives is a pleasant daydream at best and a cruel fantasy at worst. Even so, we all seem ready to embrace the mirage. That's why we get angry and feel discontent when we lose control of a situation we feel we ought to have a handle on. We act as though we've really lost something, but we never truly had it at all.

Even so, God has left a few very vital aspects of life under our control.

- We have control over our own attitudes.
- We have control over our responses to circumstances.
- We have control over our choice to seek God.
- We have control over our determination to be still before Him.
- We have control over our choice to acknowledge that He is God—and we are not!

Even though we have the power to choose in those situations, making the right choice can still be terribly difficult. For instance, we recognize that God has ultimate control over our lives and over the world, so we choose to trust Him even when we don't like or understand His ways. We loosen our tight grip and begin to hold the precious things in our lives with an open hand. We trust His plan, His ways, and His goodness more than we trust our own.

That kind of acknowledgment and trust has ushered ultimate peace into my thought closet. Peace now rests on the shelf where anger used to seethe. The same will be true for you. Unanswered questions and dissatisfaction can tempt you to raise a curled fist toward heaven. But this is the posture of anger. Open hands lifted to heaven, however, are positioned to receive. An open hand is the posture of peace and stillness. The prophet Isaiah reminds us of God's promise: "You will keep in perfect peace him whose mind is steadfast, because he trusts in you" (Isaiah 26:3).

Our trust in God is inextricably linked to our peace from God. Peace comes when we loosen our grip and let down our guard before our heavenly Father. We enjoy *shalom* when we get still in our souls before Him.

> Be still, and know that I am God (Psalm 46:10).

The original Hebrew word for *still* in Psalm 46 pictures a physical position. It's like letting your body go limp or relaxing the grip of your hand. It simply means that we quiet ourselves by acknowledging that He is God and we are not. To do that, we must first accept that He has ultimate control and we do not. That is where ultimate peace resides. Yet the pathway of peace, like a highway after a landslide, has pieces of the road that are washed away. These washouts make forward progress very, very difficult.

Washouts on the Path to Peace

Let's consider three significant washouts that will block our journey as we pursue the peace that Jesus grants us.

A Negative Mind-Set

Yes, the thoughts we allow to dominate our minds, our personal think tanks, can become major washouts on the highway to peace. The way you think is either a pothole that keeps you from calm or a bridge that gives you access to tranquility.

Some things in this life are simply hard. We don't like them, we don't want them, but we have to deal with them anyway. Often, these are conditions that legitimately warrant our frustration, such as abandonment by a spouse, harsh words from a coworker, a diagnosis of terminal illness, or some troubling, chronic physical condition.

We often assume that these situational realities in our lives are the sources of our inner anger. But the real source of anger isn't a tough circumstance or a difficult person; it's the way we choose to think about that person or circumstance. That's why we must choose a peaceful mind-set when something might fan our inner flames into rage.

Blindness isn't the source of my anger. But my *attitude about blindness* might be! I've learned to consider my blindness (or anything else that might produce anger) as a bridge.

Yes, a bridge. A bridge that takes me somewhere. A bridge that allows for progress and opens the way to new vistas along my journey.

The alternative mind-set is to think of it as an obstacle or barrier, a wall. Walls block my view. They prevent me from traveling forward. That's when they become cages, prisons. Walls are hindrances to where I really want to be, and walls really make me mad.

It's all a mind-set.

Choose wisely, my friend. The words you speak to your soul can build either bridges or walls. Building one requires just as much emotional energy as building the other, so invest wisely. The wrong mind-set is a massive sinkhole that destroys the road forward and leaves you alone in the bottom of your own bitterness. From there you can only look up and wonder where the road went and what in the world happened. But bridges allow you to pass safely over cave-ins and washouts on the highway into your future.

So what is your mind-set? Are you a bridge builder?

Anger over Adversity

Life isn't fair. My boys have reminded me of that at least a thousand times and in a thousand ways. And they're right. Blindness, cancer, betrayal, illness, injustice, demanding bosses, unexpected losses, ungrateful children, and just plain meanness...the list of inequities could fill the rest of this book. Adversity is a slippery landslide that will sweep us off our highway if we let it.

At the risk of sounding trite, here's what I have learned about this matter of adversities and hardships. Accept them. Don't let them fill you with anger. I know, I know...that sounds simplistic and not too original. But hear me out.

No one has given us an ironclad promise that life will be fair. It has never been, and it never will be. It is what it is, and it will be what it will be. Accepting that reality isn't the same as approving of that reality. It's just being real. Your depression or rage won't make the bad things go away. Bad things really do happen to good people. Innocent people can be treated poorly. Life sometimes takes a wrong turn. Evil won't go away just because it makes you mad.

This washout in the highway can stop us cold. The only way to deal with the harshness that life can bring is to face it squarely. And we have two options: anger or acceptance. Louis L'Amour, a famous Western novelist, wrote that "anger is a killing thing: it kills the man who angers, for each rage leaves him less than he had been before—it takes something from him."

Adversity is a difficult and demanding road to travel! When you allow anger to wash out your path, you will really wear yourself out. And by the time you notice, you'll be utterly spent...lost on a detour from the way of peace.

I hate suffering and injustice, and I don't discount anyone's anger over such things. I feel it too. But I also agree with Marcus Aurelius' assessment: "How much more grievous are the consequences of anger than the causes of it."

So take your tremendous passion and energy about life's injustices and use them for good—for yourself and for others. You can't often change adverse circumstances, but you can change your reaction to it. For me, accepting the adversity of blindness has become a stepping-stone of hope and encouragement for others. And along the way, slipping up behind me on my pathway, I've found an unexpected companion.

Peace.

Ask God to help you embrace what you can't avoid, accept what you don't like, and channel your passion into wise responses.

Stubborn Defiance

We don't veer off our pathway to peace because we're disabled or helpless. We skid into those highway washouts and bridgeless canyons when we are defiant. Absence of peace is not an "I can't" circumstance. It's an "I won't" choice. That's hard truth, I know, but these are words I have spoken again and again to my own soul before I started writing them for you.

Letting go of anger may seem impossible, but my friend, it's not impossible at all. Not with an all-powerful God in your corner! Guard yourself from the belief that you can't and consider that the real problem might be that you just won't! Being defiant and being disabled are vastly different.

Someone has said that anger is one letter short of danger. And it is. But danger to whom? Well, the wall in my apartment was in danger when I kicked a hole in it. And others can certainly be hurt—often the ones we love the most—by our angry words and actions. But victim number one is you! Defiance, an unwillingness to let go of anger, hurts you, my friend. It hurts you inside and out. It hurts your self-esteem and your relationships with others. It hurts your present and your future. And you are far too valuable to live like that.

The world needs the personal peace you can bring to it. But you can't clutch anger like carry-on baggage and expect to find peace.

If you want peace to prevail in your life, watch the warning signs on the highway. What is your mind-set? Is it destructive or constructive? How do you deal with adversity? With anger or with acceptance? What do you say about defiance and letting go of anger? How much of your refusal to change hurtful ways starts with "I won't" rather than "I can't"?

Recognizing these highway hazards will help you stay on the path of peace, guided by the helpful items in your thought closet.

Fire in the Closet

I have started a few fires in my attempts to cook! The worst was in an old oven in our home in Oklahoma. The oven didn't match our kitchen, and I really didn't like it at all. But it worked just fine.

That meant, of course, that ever-frugal Phil would not even consider replacing it. He wasn't concerned that it didn't match. He was most concerned that it was free. And I was blind, so it really shouldn't have bothered me either.

But it did. It really did.

Remember what I said about being a blind control freak? Well, I like my appliances to match even if I can't see them. But even I would never purposely get rid of an ugly oven this way...really!

One night I used pot holders to place a dish in the preheated oven. I carefully positioned the pan on the middle rack and closed the door. I set the pot holder on the counter and went to another room. After a few minutes, I smelled something. I made my way back to the kitchen and clearly detected the sinister scent of smoke.

I assumed some of the casserole had bubbled over and was now searing itself on the bottom of the oven. Wrong. I opened the oven door to inspect, and flames leaped out at me. This was no sauce drip, this was an inferno! What had I done?

If you are an observant reader, you noted that I laid "the pot holder" rather than "the pot holders" on the counter, right? Yes, I was cooking the other pot holder. And it didn't smell good.

Home alone, I grabbed a bowl, filled it with water, and threw it into the oven. Almost immediately, I realized I should have turned the oven off first! I had doused the flames, but now there was a terrible electrical crackling, and a strange new smell filled the room.

Oh no, I thought. *My oven is electric, and I just poured a gallon of water on those live wires.* I barely remembered hearing somewhere that flour put out electrical fires. So I pulled out a five-pound bag of flour and sent it into the oven to smother my mess.

Let's just say we ordered pizza for dinner. Then we spent the evening cleaning the doughlike substance from every inch of my kitchen, and we went shopping for a new matching stove the next day. Score!

Fires demand responses, don't they? But not just any response will do. We need to make wise responses so we can contain and extinguish the flames. Even though Jesus places peace in our thought closets, smoldering embers can remain.

We all are much like my oven inferno. We have the potential, with the wrong conditions, to explode. The apostle James expresses the same sentiment, saying, "What causes fights and quarrels among you? Don't they come from your desires that battle within you?" [1]

We all have the prospects for volcanic explosions, and we all have the potential for soul *shalom.* We all have the potential to ignite the smoldering embers within us and create a bigger fire. Anger doesn't occur outside our thought closets. We don't have to invite it in because it's there already.

So will those sparks ever go away? I'm not sure they ever do. But you can make sure peace prevails. How? By talking to yourself, of course! Here's where a little soul talk can prevent a major conflagration.

When your anger rises, what you say to yourself will either calm things down or absolutely ignite them. Those internally spoken words you use at such crucial moments will be like water or like gasoline. Water will quench the flames. Gasoline will turn them into an inferno.

So what kind of self talk do you use? What do you throw on

those emotions when they are smoldering and about to break into flame? Do you settle yourself down with soothing words of truth, or do you stoke the fire with accusations, bitterness, and self-pity?

This is well worth your time to consider so that when the dangerous moment arrives, you will have already thought through your response. What ignites your anger? What settles you down when you are mad? What do you say to yourself that brings you peace? Make your own list of "gasoline words" and "water words." Here are some of mine.

Gasoline words:

* you always...
* you never...
* you should have...
* you ought to...

Water words:

* I understand.
* I don't blame you.
* Good try.
* Way to go.
* There's always next time.
* I forgive you.

Gasoline words make things worse. When we're quick to judge, to point out flaws, and to criticize, our words make feelings grow and emotions escalate. The Bible says that "a gentle answer turns away wrath, but a harsh word stirs up anger." [2]

Do you use gasoline words when you talk to yourself? Do you use your self talk unwisely to stir up your discontent and anger? If you're not sure, think about how you speak to others. Often those who are harsh and quick to judge others turn that same flammable intolerance on themselves. Gasoline words rarely express mercy. You shouldn't speak those words to others, and you shouldn't speak them to your own soul either. Your soul needs the water of the Word to wash over your thought closet.

Water words soothe. They are pleasant to the ear and breezy to the heart. They make feelings settle down and allow emotions to find proper perspective. Water words are full of discretion, grace, and mercy. They don't condemn. They encourage and cleanse. As Solomon wrote, "A man's discretion makes him slow to anger, and it is his glory to overlook a transgression."³ Are you a woman of peaceful water words? Do you rightly speak the gentle answers of truth to your soul?

You might assume that a hard, truthful word is not a water word. Not so! Grace and truth can be hard to hear sometimes, but they do bring peace. Scalding hot water sterilizes and cold water prevents swelling. Water words are the same to our souls. They may hurt for a moment, but the result is healing and health.

I have spoken difficult and corrective water words to my soul before. I remember feeling embarrassed after saying something I shouldn't have said to a friend. Irritated at myself, I was meditating on me, myself, and lies, and I was tempted to throw some gasoline into my thought closet. *Jennifer! Open mouth, insert foot. You shouldn't have said that. Idiot! How could you have been so small?*

Those sorts of words, even if they are never spoken aloud, will only make things worse, stoking the fires of discontent, anger, and self-hatred. Instead, I sprinkled some water into my thought closet. *Jennifer, Jennifer, you said that because you felt self-conscious or insecure. But you are secure in God—you know that. You don't need to focus on yourself. Focus on Him and others. Remember how this happened and how this feels so you won't do it again.*

Corrective water words don't always feel good, but they bring wellness. Think about that. Do you appreciate yourself enough to find truth and speak it to your soul? I hope so. Don't run from water words that point out a place in your life that needs growth.

Use those cool, refreshing words to safeguard against fires in your thought closet and to nourish the barren places where you long for the fruitfulness of God's truth.

Not every hard word is a gasoline word, but every harsh word is. The true test is what those words do to the flames within you. If they ignite anger, they are gasoline. If they make peace prevail, they are water.

The words you speak to yourself—the thoughts you dwell on, receive, and personalize—can either cause anger to ignite or allow peace to prevail. Like a sentinel guarding the city to prevent an enemy attack, you must guard the door of your thought closet. You cannot allow words that ignite anger and promote discord in the door. They will make your thought closet dangerously hot.

Trading Your Anger for Peace

Thomas Merton observed that man is not at peace with his fellow man because he is not at peace with himself, and he is not at peace with himself because he is not at peace with God.

But it doesn't have to be that way.

You can trade your raging anger for peace like a river. The apostle Paul said, "Since we have been justified through faith, we have peace with God through our Lord Jesus Christ, through whom we have gained access by faith into this grace in which we now stand." [4]

When you have peace *with* God, you can have peace *from* God— the peace that Christ brings. When peace becomes the default setting on the thermostat in your thought closet, those little sparks are just that—little. When you speak words of peace, the sparks just won't grow.

So when things heat up, tell your soul to calm down.

Soul-Talk Questions to Ponder

1. Do you have any smoldering embers in your thought closet?

2. What kind of gasoline words do you speak to your soul?

3. What kind of water words do you need to add to your soul talk?

4. Do you rest in the fact that God is in control? If not, wrestle with that truth until it leads you to stillness before Him.

For even more tips and resources to keep you calm, visit MeMyselfandLies.us. You'll find additional Emerson quotes, peaceful Scriptures to place in your thought closet, and strategies for anger management.

Passages to Ponder

Everyone must be quick to hear, slow to speak and slow to anger; for the anger of man does not achieve the righteousness of God (James 1:19-20 NASB).

Be angry, and yet do not sin; do not let the sun go down on your anger (Ephesians 4:26 NASB).

The LORD gives strength to his people; the LORD blesses his people with peace (Psalm 29:11).

Better a dry crust with peace and quiet than a house full of feasting, with strife (Proverbs 17:1).

And the peace of God, which transcends all understanding, will guard your hearts and your minds in Christ Jesus (Philippians 4:7).

He who is slow to anger is better than the mighty, and he who rules his spirit, than he who captures a city (Proverbs 16:32 NASB).

Do not be eager in your heart to be angry, for anger resides in the bosom of fools (Ecclesiastes 7:9 NASB).

Now may the Lord of peace himself give you peace at all times and in every way. The Lord be with all of you (2 Thessalonians 3:16).

A SNEAK PEEK INTO LYSA TERKEURST'S THOUGHT CLOSET

I love talking to my friend Lysa because she has a way of putting into words what all we girls deal with! She is a bestselling author of books like *Made to Crave* and *The Best Yes,* but what I love most is that she doesn't just write about practical strategies to manage and overcome the feelings that often trip us up—she lives out those strategies herself. She has learned to keep the temperature down in her thought closet by using a faith filter and reminding her soul that feelings are not dictators; they are simply indicators...

"I can either filter through my feelings or my faith, and it's something I've learned I have to do quite often. If I'm filtering through my feelings, this is what I say to myself: 'Be true to yourself, Lysa!' and 'How you feel is how you must act and react.' But that has gotten me into trouble so, so many times! I mean...so, so, so, many times! Because, when we filter our experiences through our feelings, feelings are fickle and fragile, and honestly...quite often, they're deceptive.

"I think for me, the enemy uses that mantra, 'Be true to yourself...how you feel is how you must act and react,' to trip me up and make my situation even worse.

"But if I choose instead to filter what I'm dealing with through my faith—and not my feelings—my faith says, 'Rein yourself in with truth' and 'You can feel hurt, but you don't have to be hurt; you can feel angry but you don't have to be angry.'

"So one of my big quotes that I tell myself often is—I will literally speak it outloud—'Lysa, your feelings are indicators not dictators.'

"My feelings are great to indicate that there's a problem that needs to be addressed, but my feelings shouldn't dictate how I act or react."

I shall remember the deeds of the Lord;
Surely I will remember Your wonders of old.
I will meditate on all Your work
And muse on Your deeds.
Psalm 77:11-12 NASB

8

LOOK BACK

FORGET NOT HIS BENEFITS, O MY SOUL

The path of life I traveled in 2004 had two major milestones. Our oldest son, Clayton, started high school, and our youngest son, Connor, began kindergarten. As a result, our back-to-school shopping cart contained Clearasil and crayons, a scientific calculator and safety scissors, a protractor and Play-Doh!

Oh, yeah...and some Advil for me.

Having our boys ten years apart certainly kept life interesting.

Forget the Advil—I needed the strong stuff. Hand over the Starbucks!

That first day of school brought with it an assortment of emotions and left me wondering whether I should cry or celebrate. Milestones have a way of doing that, don't they? They give us occasion to look back over the road we've traveled.

Sometimes when we look back, we want to celebrate because we've come so far. At other times our backward glances bring tears of longing, pain, regret, or loss. Reviewing our milestones gives us a chance to mark progress and keep on the right path. It affords an opportunity to remember.

When my nest became emptier that school year, I began making a list of life goals. I probably should have made the list when I turned 30 because the list was longer than my life expectancy.

One thing I decided to do was to read everything C.S. Lewis wrote.

I began with *Mere Christianity* and then went on to read *Surprised by Joy*. Then I happened on an unexpected treasure. It was a delightful fantasy novel that Lewis wrote in 1943. The story caught me in its grasp.

It is *Out of the Silent Planet,* the first book in Lewis' space trilogy. Ever read it?

The View from Malacandra

Lewis begins his tale by introducing the main character, a philologist named Elwin Ransom, who is taking a walking tour of the English countryside. On his journey, he runs into some shady characters from his university days. After dinner, conversation, and a few drinks, Ransom is terrified when he realizes he's been hoodwinked by his former colleagues. He wakes up astonished to find himself in a metal ball soaring through the light-filled heavens, on his way to another world.

When the spacecraft sets down on a foreign planet called Malacandra, Ransom is introduced to a new culture and new perspectives. One such perspective embraces the unique power and significance of remembering. A friendly Malacandran alien later describes his first encounter with Ransom:

> When you and I met, the meeting was over very shortly. It was nothing. Now, it is growing something as we remember it. But still we know very little about it. What it will be when I remember it as I lie down to die; what it makes in me all my days, that is the real meeting. The other is only the beginning of it.

I love that thought! And it's not as alien as you might think.

Oscar Levant acknowledged, "Happiness isn't something you experience; it's something you remember." The real power of any moment is fully realized when it is remembered. The experience might have been painful or pleasant, but its intensity and meaning grow when we remember and reflect upon it, when we place it alongside those milestone moments we've stowed away in our thought closets.

Remembering is essential to the health of our souls. So we must tell our souls to look back often.

The Library in Your Mind

English author Aldous Huxley compared our memories to private collections of literature. Memories store great anthologies of stories that tell us who we are. They become intimate reminders of our personal histories.

Our memories hold countless pages of stories, thoughts, visual images, and perspectives. Your thought closet is like a library in your head. Imagine that it is lined with a giant wall of bookshelves chock-full with the stories of your life. When you pull a book from the shelf, it might bring laughter, a smile, or nostalgic longings for days gone by.

Another story you review might invite weeping, resentment, or regret. You might even wish you could remove it from your library.

So which memories should you look back to? Which books should you pull from the shelves to review? What should you tell your soul to remember? Here is your guiding principle: Tell your soul to look back only to what is profitable.

Profitable Painful Memories

Some memories are precious, so we can tell our souls to recall them with pleasure. But other memories bring pain, and telling your soul to remember those is difficult. Yet both can be profitable to your soul as you assign meaning to them. Profitable memories are those that add to your soul wellness rather than subtract from it. They prompt maturity and growth rather than drag you down or keep you stuck in your own immaturity. Profitable memories contribute to your personal depth and understanding. They challenge you to think broadly rather than narrow your perspective. That's why profitable recollections can be either pleasant or painful. Even hard times in our lives can add lots of wisdom to our thought closets.

When Clayton was only nine months old, he had major surgery, resulting in an obvious scar stretching from his little belly button to his side. He had an emergency condition arise called *intussusception*.

The memory is painful to me. It would be to any mother. Our tiny baby was in a fight for his life. And who can describe the fear that gripped us as we sat in the waiting room during his long surgery? Oh, but following those hours came the wondrous news that our little boy would be all right, that he would recover. We were so relieved, so thankful, so filled with joy.

As Clayton grew bigger, his scar grew smaller. But to this day, it is still detectable. I hope a tiny bit of it will always be visible, because it is an ever-present reminder from which we all can profit. As we see the painful scar, as we recall the dark day, we have cause to tell our souls the truth: God provides, God protects, we can persevere, things aren't always as they seem at first...and the list of truthful soul talk goes on and on! The painful memory is profitable because it adds to my personal peace. It reassures me that I can trust God if another difficulty comes into my life. Think about it. If I block out the painful memories of the waiting, the anxiety, and the prayers for God's mercy, I also block out Clayton's recovery, our great joy and relief, and our gratitude to the Healer.

Do you have a scar you've tried to forget because it is so painful? Pull it out from deep in your thought closet and ask God to shine the light of His peace upon it. He can make even painful memories profitable as He gives meaning to them. He will give you "beauty instead of ashes, the oil of gladness instead of mourning, and a garment of praise instead of a spirit of despair" (Isaiah 61:3).

When you assign meaning to a memory you label it as something profitable, and it adds to your life. If you don't label a painful memory with meaning, it will retain a negative connotation. It will be stripped of its potential profit and simply fall into the negative or neutral category in your thought closet if you don't label it with meaning.

I have one important disclaimer, though. When I speak of recalling painful memories, I am speaking of those you can manage. Some truly horrific memories are stowed in our thought closets and bring us utter agony—horrible situations of abuse or cruelty. My friend, if that's true for you, please know that often those kinds of memories require you to seek professional, spiritual intervention. Do that so you can be on the path of healing.

Profitable Pleasant Memories

Happy, pleasant memories can contribute to your life as you recall them. They can keep giving you joy long after the joyful event has past. You can profit from fabulous milestone memories as they grow in your thought closet, getting sweeter as they age.

Every year I watch the State of the Union address on television because I am a political junkie! And every year it has special significance for me. The speech is always fine no matter who is giving it, but that isn't what gives me such pleasure. Back in 2006, I had the privilege of attending the speech in person.

When I sat in the gallery above the Senate floor, I was struck by the history of the room. Overcome with patriotism and gratitude, I drank in everything just as a thirsty man would drink after a spell in the desert.

Now, in the following years, we just sit in front of the television set. But the funny thing is, the wonder in my heart never subsides at all. In fact, it grows every year. The memory is like a companion with whom I keep growing more deeply acquainted. The passing of time doesn't diminish the special occasion of attending the State of the Union. On the contrary, over the years that milestone memory has spent in my thought closet, it has become even more precious. Infused with nostalgia, it *grows and grows.* Lewis wrote, "You cannot study pleasure in the moment of the nuptial embrace, nor repentance while repenting, nor analyze the nature of humour while roaring with laughter." [1] Looking back allows you to really experience a past moment with even more depth and understanding. And telling your soul to look back gives present experiences even more pleasure.

Your memories are your history, your story. They are indicators of who you are, and they can influence who you hope to become.

Memories can be our best associates or our worst adversaries. Our recollections become friends when we learn from them and allow them to teach us. They turn into enemies when we avoid them, gloss over them, or ignore their existence.

Memories can be profitable because they protect us from repeating mistakes. They guard us against needless worry and serve as a grounding force in our lives. Milestones in our lives, those significant moments that shape us, can become stepping-stones on our path to a balanced soul.

So what should you remember? Remember whatever is profitable, whether good or bad. Those experiences have purpose and value beyond the remembering. Ask God's Spirit to guide you to profitable memories. Ask Him to help you wisely assign meaning to your milestones.

Forget Me Not

Sailors and soldiers in centuries past made remembrance gifts for their sweethearts and sent them home from their journeys abroad. Each relic carried a sentiment with its beads and fringes.

Many of the inscriptions read, "Forget me not."

You can imagine the lonely soldier or sailor wondering if his faraway love would forget about him in his absence and find someone else. So he sent his gift with hopes that it would serve as a sufficient reminder to "forget not" his devotion.

There is something about asking someone to "forget not." It's more than remembering. I put things on my to-do list to remember them. But to "forget not" goes a step further. The request implies remembering with both desire and duty. David told his soul to "forget not" God's benefits. When you look back at profitable memories—both pleasant and painful—you do the same. When was the last time you told your soul to "forget not"?

Our souls need such prompting. Otherwise, we can too easily focus only on today, this moment, this worry, this problem, this present reality. *Yet our memories of what God has already done are just as compelling and every bit as real.* You and I need some "forget me nots" in prominent places in our thought closets.

Now is a good time to give it a try. Say to your soul, *Soul, remember the good things God has done.* Now put the rest of your world on hold for a few moments and simply ponder the thought. If you have trouble, step outside and feel the breeze, breathe in the fresh air, feel the sunlight fall gently on your skin, or listen to the chirp of a bird or the rustle of leaves in the wind.

Look around. Take time to observe what lies just beyond the surface of your circumstances. You'll see evidence of the goodness and benefits of God. It feels good, doesn't it?

Remembering the good things of God sometimes causes you to reflect back on the bad things of life. But don't shy away from those painful memories because in those dark, difficult places, we often become more deeply acquainted with the good and comforting presence of God.

Forget Not His Benefits

That's what the psalmist said to his soul.

When I tell my soul to look back and note His goodness, my soul grabs a book from a shelf in my thought closet. I do this in a practical way by reviewing some of my journals from the past. I've heard it said that the weakest ink is stronger than the strongest memory. Of course, I don't remember who said that because I didn't write it down!

Journaling is a great way to help your soul look back. You can do it in a Moleskine notebook, in a flowery padded diary, on your computer's hard drive (that's how I do it), or in a blog. The point is to write down your soul's reflections in a place you can revisit so you can apply some practical "forgetting not."

We write these things down for the same reason that David told his soul not to forget. We are prone to forgetfulness.

In the Old Testament book of Deuteronomy, God urged His people at least eight times not to forget what He had done for them. He tells them to remember *sixteen* times. His reminders are like Post-it notes stuck on their cabinets, taped to their mirrors, and tucked in their wallets.

The title *Deuteronomy* actually means *second law.* It was an obvious reminder—God's version of a neon sign. Let's face it, we all need Post-it notes or maybe even neon signs to help us recall and assign meaning to the memories in our thought closets. I use several things to help me "forget not" what really matters. One is a ceramic turtle I keep in my jewelry box. Every time I reach for a ring to place on my finger, I run across the little turtle. He reminds me that he and I have a lot in common. He represents the turtle on a fencepost—he didn't get there by himself.

The same applies to me. I didn't get where I am by myself either. I am who I am and where I am because of God. That simple reminder keeps me from having an elevated view of myself and helps me never to forget God's work in my life.

Another little reminder I used to carry in my pocket was the worry rock my dad gave me. It was a beautiful stone with a deep thumb-sized impression in its center. My dad used to say it was from him constantly rubbing his thumb on the rock as he worried about me. He gave it to me when I was in my teens as a reminder that I could cast all my worries on God because God cared for me.

When I first began to travel and speak, I carried the special pebble in my purse or the pocket of my jacket to help ease my nerves. Whenever I'd search through my purse or put my hands in my pockets, I'd often feel the stone, and it reminded me that I didn't need to worry.

What do you use to help you remember what really matters? Do you carry photos in your wallet or phone? Do you keep Scripture verses or quotes posted in prominent places in your home or office to help you remember? These are all just simple ways to tell your soul to forget not, to look back and remember. And we all need them. We need cues to remind us of what our lives are really about.

When you figure out what you need to bear in mind, put some practical memory aids to work. These tools will prompt you to speak some healthy soul talk.

I Will Remember

I don't know if the psalmist named Asaph had Post-it notes or pebbles in his pocket, but I do know he had one accessory in his thought closet that helped him to remember—and you have the same accessory: the ability to choose.

He chose to remember, disciplined himself to remember, and willed his soul to remember. This is what he wrote:

> I will remember my song in the night;
> I will meditate with my heart,
> And my spirit ponders...
> I shall remember the deeds of the LORD;
> Surely I will remember Your wonders of old.
> I will meditate on all Your work
> And muse on Your deeds (Psalm 77:6,11-12 NASB).

Did you notice how often he said, "I will" or "I shall"? But I didn't quote the words that preceded all of the "I wills." Those were words of complaining, wondering, and worrying. Familiar? I have a tendency to do that too when I look at my past.

But the psalmist must have remembered the goodness of God in every memory because he transitioned from complaining to contemplating. Our souls are nourished when we do the same.

> I have considered the days of old,
> The years of long ago (verse 5).

Asaph moved from woes to wonder. He reminded his soul of the good things God had done. And then he began to meditate on the works of God.

Meditating is part of remembering. It reinforces what we know. Meditation is a constant stream of soul talk. It's a subconscious way of keeping our thought closets well stocked.

Do you meditate? I used to think I didn't know how to meditate until I realized I unconsciously did it all the time—I worried. Meditating on the past is a form of remembering, but meditating on the future is a form of worry. Ever thought of that? Are you good at meditating?

Are you a chronic worrier? Meditating on things that aren't true (or aren't true yet) and fixating on memories that are unprofitable are lethal kinds of meditation. Mulling over and ruminating can become unhealthy ways of meditating that reinforce negative thoughts and suppositions.

Lethal meditation will leave your thought closet cluttered with outdated memories that appear to be the latest fashions. This deceitful kind of self talk never leads to liberty. It leaves you destined to be clothed with heavy chains of bondage rather than the fashion of freedom. So do you meditate, or do you worry? If you're not sure, listen in on my conversation with my friend Alicia.

Not True Yet

My friend Alicia Britt Chole, a former atheist, is a sharp and witty author and speaker who is always full of depth and insight. In a casual conversation about her book *Anonymous: Jesus' Hidden Years...and Yours,* I asked her if her self talk had changed as she transitioned from living as an atheist to a follower of Christ.

> **ALICIA:** Coming out of atheism, I lived in a daydream world. All the time, everywhere I'd go, there was this alternative reality going on in my brain—either about the future or the past. Since I came to faith, God has severely disciplined my thoughts. I don't even have permission to daydream because of what it develops inside me. I'm not talking about harmless hopes for a bright future...a lot of my daydreams were inspired by fear. Fear had a tremendous hold on what happened in my mind—especially as a pre-believer. And so I've developed this principle: Meditation on untruth is unprofitable for the soul. So if it's not true, or not true yet, I won't allow myself to go there.
>
> **JENNIFER:** What does it mean to be "not true yet"?
>
> **ALICIA:** Okay, here's one of the things I struggled with as a newly married woman. I was constantly in this self-conversation about fear. I remember once when my husband, Barry, was supposed to be home at noon. When he wasn't, I thought, *That's interesting.* At 12:05, I thought, *Hmmm.* At 12:10, I was thinking, *I wonder if something happened.* This was before cell phones. At 12:15: *What IF something happened?* At 12:20: *Something DID happen—and it was bad.*
>
> By 12:25, I could see my husband crossing the road and getting hit by a bus. At 12:30, I could see him lying in a puddle of blood while the ambulance arrives. By 12:45, I pictured the policeman knocking at my door,

announcing that Barry is dead. At 1:00, I am on the floor weeping, thinking about my husband's funeral.

At 1:05, Barry comes walking through the door, and he's greeted by me saying, "You're alive! You're alive!"

And you see, I just spent five years of emotional energy mourning the death of a man who was stuck in traffic. I was doing this all the time and finally began to hear Father God asking me, *Do you think this is beneficial? Is it true?* I answered, *Not yet.* That's when He started planting in my soul the principle that meditation on untruth is unprofitable for the soul. And that's been the guiding force for my self talk.

JENNIFER: So your barometer is, if it's not true—or not true yet—you won't dwell on it?

ALICIA: Yes, but here's the rest of it: Even if it *is* true, will talking to myself about it change anything? And if thoughts don't get past those two filters, I will not invest any emotional or mental energy in them. It's not always easy, but it is always profitable.

JENNIFER: True, but if it's not easy, how do you make yourself do it?

ALICIA: I've learned to train my brain. Simple, practical things. I begin praying for other people—this I do the most. I focus my mental and emotional energy on making a spiritual difference in someone else's life. When possible, I open a Bible and start to read. It doesn't matter if I'm reading about the cubits in the temple or 2 Corinthians, I start reading the Word of God.

JENNIFER: It sounds like those things help you change your focus. Do they work quickly?

ALICIA: Not always, but they do work. I may struggle with a negative or unprofitable thought 100 times today. My goal is 99 tomorrow. And then 98 the next day.

JENNIFER: Does it eventually whittle down to 1 or 0?

ALICIA: Absolutely. I've seen that over the last 20-something years of walking with Jesus. There are things that were consuming in my self talk that now no longer knock on the door.

Like Alicia, we must discipline our souls to remember and meditate wisely. Along with David, we must tell our souls to "forget not" the benefits of our God. And like Asaph, we must remember, meditate, and ponder. Meditation matters and is central to remembering.

Tell your soul to look back at your milestones whether they warrant celebration or tears. Peek into your thought closet to recall the unexpected twists and turns that life's road has taken. Reminisce over even the difficult milestones, such as grave sites, storm shelters, unemployment lines, doctor's offices, police stations, or moving vans.

Meditating on God's goodness can turn even the most difficult milestones into stepping-stones on a path of gratitude, contentment, and peace. Whether your most recent milestones have caused you to shed a tear or lift a cheer, tuck them away in your thought closet and label them as spiritual markers—reminders of God's provision and presence along the way.

So, my friend, tell your soul to remember. Remember the goodness of God. Meditate on profitable truth. Ponder the meaning of those memories. Remembering allows your experiences to grant you far more than a fleeting moment of pleasure or pain.

Join me in telling your soul to "look back." When you do, you gaze into a thought closet that has been fully stocked with profitable truth worth remembering.

Soul-Talk Questions to Ponder

1. Is your thought closet full of memories that control you? If so, ask God's Spirit to help you control those memories.

2. Take some time to assign meaning to the memories in your thought closet.

3. Do you need to work on wise meditating? Think about what kind of constant self talk you engage in. Is it true? True yet? Profitable? If not, ask God's Spirit to help you control those thoughts. Review chapter 4 if you need a refresher and check out 2 Corinthians 10:4.

For some more tips and resources to help you look back, visit MeMyselfandLies.us. You'll also find some of my family photos and ways to improve your memory.

Passages to Ponder

Remember the days of old;
consider the generations long past.
Ask your father and he will tell you,
your elders, and they will explain to you
(Deuteronomy 32:7).

Remember the wonders he has done,
his miracles, and the judgments he pronounced
(1 Chronicles 16:12; Psalm 105:5).

On my bed I remember you;
I think of you through the watches of the night (Psalm
63:6).

When our fathers were in Egypt,
they gave no thought to your miracles;
they did not remember your many kindnesses,
and they rebelled by the sea, the Red Sea
(Psalm 106:7).

I remember your ancient laws, O Lord,
and I find comfort in them (Psalm 119:52).

In the night I remember your name, O Lord,
and I will keep your law (Psalm 119:55).

I remember the days of long ago;
I meditate on all your works
and consider what your hands have done
(Psalm 143:5).

Remember your Creator in the days of your youth,
before the days of trouble come
and the years approach when you will say,
"I find no pleasure in them" (Ecclesiastes 12:1).

Remember Jesus Christ, raised from the dead, descended from David. This is my gospel (2 Timothy 2:8).

Remember those earlier days after you had received the light, when you stood your ground in a great contest in the face of suffering (Hebrews 10:32).

A SNEAK PEEK INTO STORMIE OMARTIAN'S THOUGHT CLOSET

I want to be just like Stormie when I grow up! She's the author of *The Power of a Praying Woman*, and she truly is a woman of prayer who inspires me to get on my knees so I can get over my issues and get on with life! She may have sold more than 35 million books, but that's not the reason I want to be like her. I want to be like Stormie because she has learned how to take even the worst messes of her past and turn them into messages that set people free!

And it's all because she knows what to tell her soul when she looks back...

"Negative self-talk was a paralyzing struggle for me for the first 35 years of my life. From the time I was a small child, my mentally ill mother was physically and verbally abusive to me. She frequently called me filthy names I cannot repeat and locked me in a dark closet. In the closet her words played over and over in my mind. Of the words I *can* repeat, her favorites seemed to be, "You're worthless and will never amount to anything." Unfortunately, I heard her discouraging words enough to believe them, even after I realized her condition. It wasn't until after I received the Lord at 28 and learned the truth about who I am in His eyes that this began to change. With the help of God's Word and prayer, I could take charge of my mind and refuse to listen to the lies. Then I could truly come out of the darkness of my emotional closet and live in the light.

"My biggest breakthrough came when I learned I must forgive my mother completely for every bad and negative experience I had with her. It was really hard, and it did not happen overnight because each time I forgave her for something and thought it was done, something else would surface in my memory. But I kept asking God to help me forgive her completely. And He did. In the process I learned that forgiving someone does not make him or her right; it makes you free."

I will still and quiet my soul.

9

CHILL OUT

BE AT REST, O MY SOUL

Let me show you a milestone that became a stepping-stone in my thought closet. It just might be one you recognize!

On a crisp fall morning, I sat with my precious friend and writing assistant, Karen, in her upstairs office. We had worked on the manuscripts for several books together, and I loved the process of research and writing.

It was a brand-new world for me, and I was fully enjoying the exploration. I had begun writing my first book just one year earlier and now found myself on a fast track. I wasn't sure if I was driving, being driven, or a combination of the two. My travel schedule had swollen with opportunities that I didn't feel I could or should turn down.

But this was all okay with me. After all, I was growing, learning, and being stretched in the process.

Karen and I planned to work on some new book proposals that Friday while Phil was out of town. And I had decided to totally redecorate and update our bedroom while he was gone too. The painter was finishing the transformation of my boring beige walls to exciting artichoke even as Karen and I worked. I had bought the

new cranberry, mustard, and sage bedspread, curtains, and accessories the week before, and I was so excited about returning home from
my time with Karen to put the finishing touches on our bedroom.

So why did I burst into tears midsentence as we discussed the
book proposal?

I still don't fully understand the reason for the sudden cloudburst,
but I think it had a lot to do with exhaustion. Raw, unforgiving,
relentless tiredness. Not so much physical, but mental, emotional,
and spiritual. I was empty, drained, and desperate with fatigue.

The morning had begun well enough. Well, the first five minutes
of it anyway. As Karen booted up her computer, I fell silent and
began that quiet quiver we seem to adopt when we are trying hard
to compose ourselves. Karen turned her eyes from the computer
screen and fixed them on me.

"What is it?" she asked. "Are you all right?"

Well, that's all it took. Her questions were like emotional Drano,
and all that I had kept clogged inside was immediately dislodged.

"Come on," she said. "Let's get a mocha!"

The tears that began in her office continued through tea and
scones. Later she took me home and dropped me off. I barely
held my composure. Barely held it, that is, until I walked into my
bedroom and realized that the painter had not put my curtain rod
back up. In fact, he had removed all the nails and painted over the
holes! The furniture was in the middle of the room.

That did it. That *really* did it. I burst into a Niagara of tears.

Alone, I couldn't hang the rod. I couldn't move the furniture,
and I couldn't hammer the nails back into the exact places where
the pictures had hung. I remember sitting on the middle of my
bedroom floor between a bedpost and a mirror, leaning against the
dresser and feeling desperate.

It wasn't the condition of my bedroom; it was the condition of
my life that caused me to cry while considering book proposals and
to fall apart when discovering a disassembled bedroom. I just wanted

to crawl into the bed in the middle of my room with my faded green comforter and sleep, sleep, sleep.

That's when my friend Christin called.

"How's the bedroom?" she asked.

Of course, I couldn't even get out an answer because of crying. "I'm coming right over," she said, and she hung up before I could say anything else. She arrived a few minutes later with hammer and nails. Somehow, between my sobs she heard over the telephone, she was able to detect that I needed some hammering.

Christin pressed and hung the curtains and then helped me hang each picture. She consoled me as she dragged the dresser and tidied things up. By the time she left, my bedroom was intact, my soul was on the mend, and I couldn't thank God enough for the friends He had given me.

Anatomy of a Meltdown

My sudden meltdown really wasn't much of a mystery. I was weary. Soul weary.

I like the way one writer states it: "Each soul is like a carefully wired circuit breaker that can function splendidly when operating according to its design but which, when overloaded, crackles with the sparks and shorts of a system bearing more than it can hold." [1]

I was overloaded.

The time had finally arrived when my fatigue became more powerful than my fortitude. You've been there too, right? It's that moment when you can't crank the engine anymore. It's just done…out of gas! Instead of telling my soul to chill out, I was into some dangerous revving up. Solomon put it like this: "Better is a handful of quietness than two hands full of toil and a striving after wind." [2]

The whole experience taught me that speaking rest to my soul was something more than a weekend proposition. Speaking rest to my soul should be part of my daily conversation.

I know. Life is busy. The demands are great, and we seem to

have no time for rest. So much of our self talk is directed at revving ourselves up. "Come on, Jennifer, one more event, one more book, one more goal, one more phone call, one more proposal, one more trip, one more, one more..." Excessive revving up, however, only leads to petering out. All that's left is "no more...no more...no more."

Sister, daily we must tell ourselves to chill out.

We set ourselves up for failure when we don't speak rest to our souls. Researchers define burnout as "a state of physical, emotional, and mental exhaustion caused by long-term involvement in emotionally demanding situations." [3] We are all involved in emotionally demanding situations. For some of us, it's our jobs. For others of us, it's family responsibilities. For you, it might be both—and more.

I remember hearing Chuck Swindoll quote some on-fire zealot who declared, "I'd rather burn out than rust out!" And to that Dr. Swindoll replied, "What's the difference? Either way, you're out!" Amen. Preach it, Chuck!

Burnout doesn't occur just because your life has demands that you resent or dread. Oh no, even good things you enjoy can be emotionally demanding. If those emotional demands last a long time though, without a rest now and then, burnout is inevitable. When we aren't rested, we burn out, wear out, and even freak out (as I did).

If we don't tell our souls to chill out every now and then, we are also subject to attack.

An Easy Target

That's what happened to the nation of Israel. The Israelites learned about the high price of exhaustion when they made their exodus from Egypt. Talk about emotionally and physically exhausted! God said to Moses, "Remember what the Amalekites did to you along the way when you came out of Egypt. When you were weary and worn out, they met you on your journey and cut off all who were lagging behind" (Deuteronomy 25:17-18).

Who lagged behind? The ones who were feeble, tired, and worn out, the ones who desperately needed rest.

This enemy didn't go for the strong ones or the ones up-front, marching ahead in victory and confidence. No, this enemy, like the enemy of our souls, went for the weary, the stragglers, those who were tired and barely hanging on. That's the age-old strategy of coyotes, wolves, panthers…and the ruthless "roaring lion."

When we are physically and emotionally spent and worn, we become susceptible to the enemy's attack. We become easy targets, sitting ducks. Our enemy attacks us with despair, depression, illness, impatience, and all other kinds of stuff…all results of a fatigued soul and body. Speaking rest to our souls is critical.

Rest isn't only for our tired bodies, though. Weary souls need it too—our wills, our minds, and our emotions. But sometimes the silent signals of exhaustion from deep within our thought closets are more difficult to recognize than our bodies' cries for physical rest. Our minds must receive rest. Our wills must experience rest. Our emotions must engage in rest. As the psalmist said, "Surely I have composed and quieted my soul; like a weaned child rests against his mother, my soul is like a weaned child within me."[4]

My friend, that kind of rest is a *decision.*

We must choose for our wills to take a break from striving, for our minds to quiet the noise of thought, and for our emotions to detangle our knotted feelings. I wish "soul rest" automatically happened when the sun went down. But soul rest only occurs when we speak rest to our souls. True rest is a soul Sabbath, a forever Sabbath.

Forever Sabbath

As I discussed paint samples with a friend, she commented that I was the most colorful blind woman she had ever known. I quipped back that I was actually the *only* blind woman she had ever known.

But even so, she's probably right. For someone who can't see, colors are really important to me. I have vivid memories of the palate of colors I once saw. I remember fondly how pale and delicate yellow looked as it caressed the petals of a buttercup. I loved the many faces of red—warm and cozy splashed on the skin of a tomato or intense and passionate highlighted on a fire engine. As a young teen, I began collecting cobalt blue Depression glass just because I had never seen such a striking shade of blue. It even made a bottle of milk of magnesia look appealing.

I've carried this love of color along with me, and now I choose to see my friends through the many hues in my mind's eye.

Here's what I mean. My friend Melinda is the color yellow...soft and tender, warm and inviting. My friend, Kathryn, on the other hand, is bright red. She's bounding with energy, passionate, and vivacious. Then there's my friend Karen. She is green. Not a dark and hearty hunter green—she's somewhere between the soothing shade of an avocado and the warm hue of an artichoke. She's calming, settled, and peaceful.

Some days I need the color red to invade my life. I need Kathryn's passion to light my fire. Other days I am drawn to the warmth and tenderness of my friend Melinda. And still other days I just want to sit awhile with Karen. I need her calm to quiet my chaos. I long for her restfulness to unruffle my rumpled feelings.

If God were a color, what would it be?

Certainly He is more vibrant than a rainbow, more intense than the deepest baltic blue. He's more brilliant than ruby red, more dazzling than amethyst. But I think I see God on most days as green—emerald, jade, sage. He's like a calming, lush green pasture. And isn't it interesting how the book of Revelation reveals that an emerald rainbow encircles God's throne. [5] To me, God is the color of peace and rest. Maybe that's because God *is* the essence of peace and rest.

If you read the Genesis creation account, you'll be reminded that each of the six days had a beginning and an end.

God called the light "day," and the darkness He called "night." And there was evening, and there was morning—the first day...

God called the expanse "sky." And there was evening, and there was morning—the second day...

And there was evening, and there was morning—the third day...

And there was evening, and there was morning—the fourth day...

And there was evening, and there was morning—the fifth day...

God saw all that He had made, and it was very good. And there was evening, and there was morning—the sixth day. [6]

Each of the six days of creation clearly had a beginning and an end; evening and morning. But the seventh day, the day God rested, was different. The Bible records no beginning and no end of that day.

By the seventh day God had finished the work He had been doing; so on the seventh day He rested from all His work. And God blessed the seventh day and made it holy, because on it He rested from all the work of creating that He had done (Genesis 2:2-3).

In other words, God did not begin to rest, nor did He cease to rest. Ancient rabbinic scholars believed this was because the nature of God is eternal rest.

Take that in for just a minute. Let it settle in your mind. Doesn't it make you want to paint the walls of your thought closet the color green? That thought is like a deep, relaxing, cleansing breath. It makes my tension give way to tranquility. Our God is rest, and He offers His rest to us. He holds out a forever Sabbath to you and me because He is a forever Sabbath God.

You see, rest isn't just what God *did*. Rest is who God *is*.

Rest means we quiet ourselves next to the One who not only gives peace but who is the Prince of Peace. He makes us to lie down in green pastures, and He leads us beside the still waters. [7] His rest causes us to cease our striving and receive His serenity.

When my friend Vicki talks about her hopelessness and desperation during the 1960s, she describes the turmoil of her soul. Lonely. Lost. Confused. Finally at the point of suicide, in utter despair one afternoon she laid her eyes on a Bible. She grasped it only long enough for it to fall open to the words of Jesus. "Come to me, all you who are weary and burdened, and I will give you rest."[8]

Uttering a desperate but hushed, "That's what I need," Vicki found rest. Actually, she *met* rest, for she met Jesus, and her life has never been the same.

My friend, have you met rest? Just like Vicki, you can also utter a simple "That's what I need," and He will come to you. He truly will make it well with your soul, cleanse you, and change your heart. Simply believe that He is who He says He is and receive His forgiveness and new life. Trade in your fatigue for faith. (Please see appendix 2 for a simple prayer to help you do this.)

He is our forever Sabbath. He makes an offer to the weak and feeble, the worn-out and burned-out, the weary and heavy laden. He offers rest for your soul. It is yours to receive. I know it's hard to remain in the place of rest! Life gets busy, events domino, our nerves fray, and...well, you know how *that* goes. In the words of Muppet philosopher Kermit the Frog, "It's not easy being green."

Even so, the Bible gives us a plan to remain in God's rest. The way I figure it, if King David, a man so close to God's heart, had to discipline his soul to rest, so do you and I.

What David Said to His Soul

In Psalm 131, David acknowledged that his soul needed rest. He might have felt zapped emotionally, worn-out from pondering, or weary from the demands of leadership. Our clue that he needed rest comes from the way he opens his psalm. Evidently faced with information overload and lots of life quandaries, he simply poured out his soul to God.

> Lord, my heart is not proud, nor my eyes haughty;
> Nor do I involve myself in great matters,
> Or in things too difficult for me (Psalm 131:1-2 NASB).

We too can clue in that our souls need rest just by taking an honest look at our own lives. Take a deep breath and see if this might be similar to some memory in your thought closet:

> You grab your laptop, iPad, cell phone, and keys. Jumping in your car, you speed along with the rest of the commuters to work. You make a quick stop at Starbucks where, while in line, you text your teenager and then chat with your mom on your cell phone, pause just long enough to order a mocha (grande, skinny, no whip, extra shot, extra hot) from a clerk who swiftly hands you the caffeine-charged drink so he can scurry to the next customer while you, still on the phone and losing no momentum, jog to a corner table to access the high-speed Internet connection to check the news, your e-mail, and the weather, and then to shop and pay a few bills before you race back to your car so you won't be late for work…

Whew! No wonder we're tired. And if the pace doesn't make you tired, the amount of information thrown at you can leave you fatigued. In 2003 alone, enough new information was generated to fill a stack of books 30 feet tall for each of the more than six billion people on earth. [9]

I don't think my iPad and I can keep up.

That kind of pace and that amount of information can create soul insomnia. No rest. That's why we, like David, must speak rest to our souls. David's response to his information overload and his life quandary was to engage in the discipline of rest. He told his soul to put his thoughts, his decisions, and even his feelings on hold for a while and rest rather than rev! "Find rest, O my soul, in God alone," he wrote in Psalm 62:5.

Our souls don't find rest in our quick pace or information accumulation. Our souls ultimately find rest in God.

Sometimes we're so consumed by the pace we keep that we don't even notice our soul weariness. We might even imagine a weird sort of relief because we have accomplished so much. But being distracted by our schedules and relieved by accomplishing a lot are not the same as being truly rested in our souls.

Does your soul find rest in marking things off your list? Or do you find your rest, as David did, in God alone? True rest is found in the forever Sabbath.

Another psalmist also found rest when he talked to his soul. We don't know his name, but we can relate to his psalm.

> I love GOD because he listened to me,
>   listened as I begged for mercy.
> He listened so intently
>   as I laid out my case before him.
> Death stared me in the face,
>   hell was hard on my heels.
> Up against it, I didn't know which way to turn;
>   then I called out to GOD for help:
> "Please, GOD!" I cried out.
>   "Save my life!"
> GOD is gracious—it is he who makes things right,
>   our most compassionate God.
> GOD takes the side of the helpless;
>   when I was at the end of my rope, he saved me.
> I said to myself, "Relax and rest.
>   GOD has showered you with blessings.
>   Soul, you've been rescued from death;
>   Eye, you've been rescued from tears;
>   And you, Foot, were kept from stumbling"
> (Psalm 116:1-8 MSG).

This ancient Hebrew songwriter is reminding his soul of God's goodness. He tells his soul to rest because "the LORD has dealt bountifully with you" (verse 7 NASB). The psalmist teaches us to rest by recognizing that God is the One who deals with us, and when He does, He goes over the top in His provision.

> His protection is reliable.
> He answers us when we call.
> He is gracious and "preserves the simple" (verse 6 NASB).

Wouldn't you love to know the story behind Psalm 116? I sure would! The story is there; you can count on it. All of us have a story. The writer here had clearly been delivered from great harm. Although we're not told the specific danger he faced, we do know that he invited his soul to rest. And he says he can have that kind of rest because of the goodness of God.

Could you write your own psalm of gratitude to God? Can you recount the way you have been delivered from harm? It might be deliverance from your own destructive thoughts, protection from hurt, or even the blessing of being born in a free country. Think about it. How has God dealt bountifully with you? Instead of speeding through your routine, ponder this thought and list how God has been gracious to you.

Listing the goodness of God on your behalf will prompt you to rest. Because God is good, we can rest.

I love that. Let's take a nap.

Yes to Rest, No to the Rest

God's forever Sabbath gives us rest, but it's up to us to take it.

> Therefore, since the promise of entering his rest still stands, let us be careful that none of you be found to have fallen short of it (Hebrews 4:1).

We must say *yes* to His rest. Can I be honest? To say yes to rest, we must say no to other things. I don't like that any more than you probably do, but chances are if you say yes more than no, you need rest.

Here's something else that's not easy to hear, but it's true. No other person can look out for you as well as you can. Other people will always have a wonderful plan for your life, but you are the only person who is an expert on you. You and I are responsible for setting personal priorities, using our resources wisely, and learning how to make room for rest. My friend Robin McGraw has written beautifully about the importance of making choices to take care of yourself. In her book *Inside My Heart,* she writes with such admiration about her own mother.

> That precious woman never put herself first. She also never took care of herself, which is why she died of a catastrophic heart attack at the age of fifty-eight...I loved my mother and I have carried her legacy of love and devotion into my relationship with my children. But I have also chosen to reject the legacy of self-neglect...that is why I take care of myself...so my body doesn't fall apart before it has to. That's exactly what my mother would have wanted for me even if she didn't do it for herself.

She's right. We should take care of ourselves—and that includes rest.

This does not mean we should be selfish, yet we are responsible to take care of ourselves. So find a reasonable balance and defend it fervently.

Ultimately, burnout is our own fault. I can only say that because I still bear the singe of former meltdowns and burnouts. (Sometimes I still think I can smell the smoke!) I have always had trouble saying no because I don't like to let anyone down. But in saying yes too often, I let myself down. And consequently, I let down the people who need me most, like my kids and my husband. *No* is a word that should go easily out the door of your thought closet—with wisdom as its guide.

Would you drive your car if the gas tank was on empty? Of course not. But how often do you keep on driving yourself even when you are empty? Benjamin Franklin once said, "He who can take rest is greater than he that can take cities."

Do you know why he compares the ability to rest with world domination? Because both require discipline. We must discipline ourselves to rest—emotionally, mentally, and physically.

My dear friend Lori Salierno told me about a great formula she learned from Pastor Rick Warren concerning rest.

> Divert daily.
> Withdraw weekly.
> Abandon annually.

What a practical way to tell your soul to maintain balanced rest. Here's how I put this to use and discipline myself to rest.

A Game Plan for Restoring Rest

Divert Daily

Each day, I choose a temporary diversion—mental, emotional, or physical.

Sir John Lubbock wrote, "Rest is not idleness, and to lie sometimes on the grass on a summer day listening to the murmur of water or watching the clouds float across the sky is hardly a waste of time."

Sometimes it's listening to a book, sometimes it's a 15-minute power nap, and sometimes it's a leisurely walk or a phone call to a friend. Sometimes just a long shower or utter silence is the diversion I need.

What about you? How can you divert daily?

Withdraw Weekly

To withdraw weekly means that you take time each week to pull back from your busy life. Just as the amount you can withdraw from a bank account depends on how much money you have to start with, so it is with your time. You may be able to withdraw for a whole day of rest and recreation. Or you may only be able to afford a few hours. The point is that you practice this discipline every week.

Some weeks I can only afford a few hours, so I use them wisely. I remove myself from anything that represents work to me. I am able to rest when I am removed from places of responsibility like my messy kitchen, my crowded in-box, and my iPhone.

How about you? How can you withdraw weekly? What can you do to grant yourself a soul Sabbath? "Sundays," S.W. Duffield said, are "quiet islands on the tossing seas of life," and our souls need a weekly Sabbath to provide a respite from the pace of life—whether it's on Sunday or not!

Abandon Annually

A real vacation—a once a year getaway—ushers in freedom from your busy schedule, liberty from fatigue. In fact, the Latin word *vacatio* means freedom.

Whoo-hoo! Don't feel badly if this is hard for you. It's hard for me too. Sometimes it's difficult to carve out the time. Sometimes it's hard to spend the money. And sometimes there is simply no time and no money. Just remember that a vacation doesn't necessarily have to be a cruise or trip to the mountains. It can simply consist of a weekend at home watching movies and ordering pizza.

Just plan some time each year to abandon your regular routine, your long to-do lists, and your jam-packed life. You might even get really radical and leave your cell phone behind—or at least muzzle it.

Telling yourself to rest involves telling yourself how to rest. What is a vacation to someone else may be pure mental strain or emotional drain to you. Have you learned what brings you rest? Determine what is restful for you. Your definition may be different from others, and that's okay.

God commanded the ancient Israelites to observe the Sabbath every seven days. And they were even instructed to give their land a rest every seven years. My friend, if the dirt needs a rest so it can continue to be fruitful, so do you. So tell your soul to chill out!

Soul-Talk Questions to Ponder

1. Do you need to speak rest to your soul?

2. What brings your soul rest?

3. In what areas of your life do you need to rest instead of rev?

4. List ways you can divert daily and withdraw weekly. Write down your plan to abandon annually (vacation) this year.

For more tips and resources to help you chill out, visit MeMyselfandLies.us. You'll also learn how to write a psalm of gratitude and discover fun ways to divert, withdraw, and abandon!

Passages to Ponder

Return to your rest, O my soul,
For the LORD has dealt bountifully with you
(Psalm 116:7 NASB).

Take My yoke upon you and learn from Me, for I am
gentle and humble in heart, and you will find rest for
your souls (Matthew 11:29 NASB).

He said to them, "Come away by yourselves to a secluded
place and rest a while." (For there were many people
coming and going and they did not even have time to
eat) (Mark 6:31 NASB).

The LORD replied, "My Presence will go with you, and I
will give you rest" (Exodus 33:14).

"You shall work six days, but on the seventh day you shall
rest; even during plowing time and harvest you shall rest"
(Exodus 34:21 NASB).

A SNEAK PEEK INTO MARGARET FEINBERG'S THOUGHT CLOSET

Margaret is a self-described "hot mess" and she's a blast to be around. She's a bestselling author of books, Bible studies, and coloring books for grown-ups! She writes, she speaks, she travels, she is a wife...deep breath...the woman is busy. And to add to the busy hot mess mix, she had a big fight with breast cancer, and she fought back with joy. If anybody understands the value of speaking rest to our souls, it's my friend Margaret, so I'm so glad she opened the door of her Thought Closet to give us a look inside.

"Tiredness is my kryptonite. Someone asked me years ago, "What causes you to sin?" My answer, without hesitance, "Lack of sleep." When I burn the candle at both ends and in the middle, when I fail to care for my body, I become monster crankypants. When I'm tired, I become short with others and myself. Even worse, the tiniest issues are magnified times 100. Every little deal becomes a huge deal. Grace vanishes. Peace disappears. Joy slips out the backdoor.

"The clue my soul needs rest is when I need caffeine past 11:00 AM. That's when I'm in trouble. I'm pushing my body too far. To prevent burn out, I need to make time to exercise, do fun activities with friends, and be diligent with bedtime even though I really want to stay up and watch one more episode on Netflix.

"When I'm alert enough to recognize my fatigue, I tell myself aloud: 'You are not in your right mind to think about this or respond to this. Go to bed. Reconsider in the morning.' When I verbalize those words, they help me shut down my mind to get the rest I need to see life, God, and others more clearly.

"I've been learning to be more gracious and kind to myself. This is not just how Christ treats me—it's also how Christ wants me to treat others. Loving others requires me to love myself.

"Scripture is so helpful for this. So is laughter. Learning to celebrate our humanness is a wonderful party once you learn to throw it!"

Who I am and what I struggle with are not the same thing.

10

PRESS ON

MARCH ON, O MY SOUL

In 1991 I was invited to sing the national anthem for an Atlanta Braves game against the Los Angeles Dodgers. Prior to that warm July evening, I had only sung the national anthem once publicly—at the opening of the Little League season in West Palm Beach, Florida. Let's just say that first experience was a whole lot less intimidating.

"The Star-Spangled Banner" is a stirring, wonderful song, but no one has ever claimed it's easy to sing. I was *so* nervous. I rehearsed madly, consumed bottles of Maalox...and then it was time to step out on the field. A reverent hush fell upon the stadium as the players removed their caps and Old Glory flapped in the wind.

I began. "Oh, say can you see..."

So far, so good. My voice filled the massive stadium. I could hear it reverberating back to me with every note. But then, something unexpected happened. As I came to the line "and the rockets' red glare," I choked and gagged. Glottal shock! Have you ever heard of it? Well, 47,000 baseball fans could tell you exactly what it sounds like.

Glottal shock makes the singer momentarily voiceless.

I choked on "glare" and heard myself gag over giant speakers reverberating throughout the stadium.

In that moment, time stood still. As if in slow motion, I could see 47,000 faces slowly contorting into confused and shocked expressions. I wanted to evaporate. I wanted to drown in a sea of Maalox.

But I couldn't. I had to finish the song. Making my recovery, I finished strongly as I belted out "and the home of the brave!" The stadium erupted in applause, and I nearly melted in sweet relief. I was so glad that it was over.

As Phil walked me off the field, he said, "Way to go, honey. Way to recover." When I met up with my folks, my dad told me how proud he was, and my mom echoed the same. As I ran into friends, they were generous with their compliments. But all I could think about was the glottal shock.

That one stadium-sized mistake.

The broken word, *glare,* replayed over and over in my mind.

Do you know how many words are in our national anthem? To save you the singing and counting, I'll fill you in. There are 82. And I sang 81 words well.

Even so, I couldn't hear the applause. I couldn't hear my parents' compliments or my husband's consoling words or my friends' congratulations. All of the positives were overwhelmed and overshadowed by that one sour note. I was humiliated and haunted by my mistake.

Finally, after several days of self-scrutiny, I told myself to focus on the 81 words I sang well rather than the one word I choked on. One wrongly sung word doesn't justify quitting—not for me and not for you!

Douglas MacArthur once said, "Age wrinkles the body; quitting wrinkles the soul." Does your soul ever get wrinkled? Are you prone to quitting when things don't turn out the way you hoped? If so, welcome to the human race. Running that race makes us weary, and sometimes we want to just sit it out for a while.

That's the time when a little soul talk is in order. Those are the moments when we must speak truth to our souls and say, *Press on.* That will put a little perseverance in your thought closet!

Practical Perseverance

One school night I found my high schooler, Clayton, lying on his floor when he was supposed to be finishing a big English project.

"What's going on?" I asked in disbelief. "What about your portfolio? Are you already done?"

He responded with a groan. "Mom, I'm just overwhelmed. This is too much. I'm too tired. There's not enough time. I just can't do it."

He was paralyzed by his project. It seemed bigger than he was, and instead of forging forward, he was ready to quit. I got down on the floor with him, feeling helpless to motivate him. No pep talk from Mom would change a thing for him that night. And that's the raw, hard truth. When you're low on hope and dogged by failure, when your motivation is running on fumes, you need more than happy talk.

You need a first step out of your dilemma.

Here's the way I made perseverance practical for him that night—and it's the way I make it practical for me. "March on, O my soul" isn't just a motivational speech or an abstract concept. To march anywhere, you need to put one foot in front of the other. You need a concrete, step-by-step, executable plan. Here's what I mean.

Turn Your Feelings into Action

If you feel overwhelmed because a project is due, *do* the project. Yes, I know that sounds too simple. But sometimes real answers *are* simple. If a particular circumstance intimidates you, take a deep breath and confront the circumstance. Instead of ruminating about your feelings, *do* something—even if it seems a small, inconsequential something. Get up off the floor. Pick up a pen. Lift up your chin. Sing the next note. Open a document on your computer and type the first word. Be like Peter getting out of the boat and walking on the storm-churned sea. He threw one leg over the edge of the boat and put his full weight on H_2O—his eyes locked on Jesus.

Steady, small actions will slowly reduce the big feeling that is paralyzing you. All feelings are real, but they aren't all based on reality, and they certainly aren't all productive! So instead of spending more of your precious emotional energy lying on the floor and pondering how overwhelmed you feel, get up and take action.

Write a to-do list and then do one thing on that list. Do what you dread; tackle the very thing that terrifies you. Turn your feelings into action. Someone wisely observed, "Nobody trips over mountains. It is the small pebble that causes you to stumble. Pass all the pebbles in your path, and you will find you have crossed the mountain."

Affirm Your True Identity

Recognize that who you are and what you struggle with are not the same thing. Just because you have failed at something doesn't mean you are a failure. As Reggie Jackson put it, "Home run hitters strike out a lot."

In late 1918, Walt Disney tried to enlist in the military but was turned away because he was underage. This was just the first of many false starts that awaited him. Rather than accepting defeat, Disney joined the Red Cross, and for a year he drove an ambulance in France. Unlike most ambulances, which were camouflaged, his was decorated with cartoon characters.

When he got home, he began producing short animated films for local businesses in Kansas City. It didn't work out. His business folded, and he lost every penny of his savings. Bankrupt and without prospects at the age of 22, Disney didn't give up. Packing up his unfinished projects, he headed for sunny California, the land of opportunity. With nothing to lose except his determination, he joined forces with his brother Roy and got a loan. They set up shop in their uncle's garage...and the rest is history.

What if 16-year-old Walt had decided he was just too young to do anything useful? What if he'd given up on his dream after his failure in Kansas City? What if he had allowed bankruptcy to define him? What if he'd decided to quit when he surveyed the dim, unglamorous, and seemingly dead-end surroundings of his uncle's garage?

Put simply, what if he'd quit? No Disney World. No Donald Duck. No Cinderella movie. Not even one Dalmatian on film! What we would have missed!

The same applies to you, my friend. If you quit, the world will be lacking what you alone bring to it. Most of us sing 81 words well, but we too often focus on the one mistake. And focusing on the mistakes makes us want to give up. I guarantee that you have done a whole lot more things right in your life than you can even count. Big mistakes matter, oh yes, but so do small triumphs. Speak truth to your soul about who you really are.

That kind of soul talk will always begin with *I am*. Remember, *I am* is not the same as *I feel*. Don't let feelings define you; let who you are define your feelings. I hope your thought closet is full of truthful "I ams" based on who He is. (See appendix 1 for reminders of who you are.)

What you do and how you feel may loom large on your radar. But what really counts is who you are. Determine your true identity and then act upon it. Don't let the struggle define you; use your true identity to properly define your struggle. Make your adversary your friend. Let it help you prove who you are rather than deplete you and drag you along its path of despair. Make your overwhelming project your friend. Let it teach and strengthen you rather than control you.

American author James Albert Michener wrote, "Character consists of what you do on the third and fourth tries."

Speak Truth to Your Soul

A wise penguin in the movie *Happy Feet* declared that "triumph is just trying with a little *oomph!*" I love that. In *The Spiritual Life*, Walter Elliott wrote, "Perseverance is not a long race; it is many short races, one after another." Both the author and the penguin make a wise point. What you invest in pays off. In other words, what you feed grows, and conversely, what you starve dies.

If you continue to feed your feelings of failure and defeat, those dark emotions will grow, creeping across your soul like long winter shadows. If you continue to feed your low self-esteem with *I can't* or *It's too hard for me,* your low self-esteem will grow. But if you begin to starve those things, they will slowly die.

So how do you starve those feelings and struggles? Speak truth to your soul. When you feel a big *I can't* coming on, starve it by showering it with the truth: "I can do all things through Christ who strengthens me."[1] When you feel like giving up, starve that thought with the truth: "We are not of those who shrink back."[2]

Remember my conversation with Patsy Clairmont from chapter 3? She showed us how we can refuse that wrong self talk, replace it with truth, and then repeat the process for as long as it takes.

What are you feeding? Is it time for you to withhold nutrition and let that damaging self talk die? Abraham Lincoln said, "I am a slow walker, but I never walk backward." So, my friend, don't turn back. Walk on, slowly but surely.

Exercise Discipline

Discipline is hard, but despair is much harder. Both can be very unpleasant, so choose the most profitable unpleasant experience. And of the two, discipline is the most profitable. Despair just continues to wrinkle your soul, but discipline is like working out. It might not feel good, but it feeds your self-esteem and makes you productive.

May I be a little blunt here? Most of the time when we say *I can't,* we are really saying *I won't.* Disability rarely hinders us as much as defiance.

Discipline should be exercised in tiny pieces, not big chunks. Lucretius said, "The drops of rain make a hole in the stone not by violence but by oft falling." Small, daily disciplines can develop a sturdy soul—strong and protected from the crushing effects of despair.

My friend, that's why a woman who speaks truth to her soul tells her soul both to chill out and to press on. Sometimes rest is more important than revving up, and sometimes pressing on is more important than pulling back.

The book of Exodus reveals that when the Israelites were cornered by the pursuing Egyptians, they were seized with panic. Instinct probably sent them into the "fight or flight" mode—and they were ready to scatter like a flock of pigeons.

That's when Moses commanded, "Do not be afraid. Stand still, and see the salvation of the LORD." Yet just a couple of verses later, the Lord said, "Tell the Israelites to move on." [3]

Sometimes we need to stand still (and chill) while we wait on God. And sometimes we need to move on, to get up and start marching.

When you invite God's Spirit to guide you, when you receive wisdom to help you monitor your thought closet, the result will be knowing when to hum Brahms' "Lullaby" and when to whistle the *William Tell* overture. "Hi ho, Silver!" The important thing is to keep marching on. Never quit even if you sit out for a spell—keep right on singing.

March On, O My Soul

The prophet Deborah led Israel when they were enslaved by a ruthless Canaanite king. His military commander, Sisera, rode roughshod over the Hebrews.

Hearing from God that the time was right to throw off the chains of slavery, Deborah commanded her general, Barak, to muster his army. The plan was for him to lead a force of 10,000 men while Deborah's smaller force marched in plain sight of Sisera's army, luring them smack into Barak's men!

Deborah was ready to press on because she had heard from God Himself. Barak, however, wasn't so sure. And can we blame him?

Facing a daunting task—particularly one that involves risk, sacrifice, and pain—can make the best of us want to wave a white flag. Maybe Barak thought his militia would probably be defeated and humiliated for yet another generation. That would be a pretty good reason for him to quit even before he began. We've all faced enemies and battles that reveal our frailty and make us feel feeble, overwhelmed, unequipped, and ready to turn tail.

In spite of his shakiness, Barak stepped up to the challenge. But he refused to go without Deborah. She agreed, but under one condition: When the Israelite army won, Barak would not be given credit for the victory. Instead, the victory would be credited to a woman. (Hum the *Rocky* theme song here.)

Let the battle begin! Deborah sent Barak to initiate the battle, and "at Barak's advance, the LORD routed Sisera...and Sisera abandoned his chariot and fled on foot" (Judges 4:15).

In other words, Sisera ran for his life, or as my Connor would say, "He ran away squealing like a little girl."

Utter celebration swept through the people of Israel. The victory had been won! They were free! And in response to this stunning victory, Deborah and Barak broke into song.

Victory Song

The new hit song swept across the liberated land. The lyrics are recorded in Judges 5. In verse 21, Deborah confidently proclaims, "March on, my soul; be strong."

In the midst of Deborah's song, she spoke perseverance to her soul. Well, actually she sang to her soul. I love that thought because I too sometimes sing to myself. Do you?

Note that this soul-talk reminder to press on is tucked within the lyrics of a victory song. We often think that we most need to speak perseverance to our souls when we are on the brink of defeat, at the end of our ropes, or in the midst of glottal shock! Of course, speaking truth to our souls then is essential, but it is no less essential in a surge of sudden prosperity.

Why? Because if we keep telling ourselves to persevere when we're winning, we'll sing the same song to our souls when victories are hard to find.

The moments following great victories may be the most vulnerable moments you face. After persevering and speaking strength to our souls, we tend to set that all aside to bask in the warm glow of sweet success.

We relax. We let down our guard. We dim the light in our thought closets and slip life into cruise control. And we are in peril beyond our understanding. As Solomon wrote, "A little extra sleep, a little more slumber, a little folding of the hands to rest—and poverty will pounce on you like a bandit; scarcity will attack you like an armed robber." [4]

That's the lesson of Deborah's song. Yes, by all means sing songs of strength to your soul when you're outnumbered, outmaneuvered, and outgunned. But don't stop after you have won the battle, when you've gotten the answered prayer, the promotion, the opportunity, the success. Keep right on singing, *March on, my soul, be strong! Don't stop now. Don't falter.*

The habit of perseverance will protect us after the battle, after the triumph, when we could easily have an "Elijah episode."

The Downside of Winning

Another prophet, Elijah, was ready to sing his last note—not because he was defeated, but because he had just won!

Beneath a broom tree in the desert, he prayed, "I have had enough, LORD…Take my life." [5]

Do you know when he uttered such weak, pitiful words? It was right after an earthshaking mountaintop experience on the peak of Mount Carmel. He had just called fire down from heaven and seen his adversaries fall to their knees. Then he had prayed for God to send rain, and the heavens opened with a thundering deluge. He was firing on all cylinders, but soon he had a meltdown. Elijah went from the height of the mountain to the depths of the valley.

The same man who stood bravely before 450 prophets of Baal ran like a coward from one woman who threatened to kill him.

Exhausted (which is often how we feel after a mountaintop experience), Elijah curled up in a fetal position under a tree in the desert and slept until an angel woke him up and made him eat. He was strengthened by that food, and he went on to do God's work.

Notice with me that he wanted to quit—not before the battle, not during the battle, but *after* the battle. Yes, he was being pursued by Jezebel, who wanted to get her long, pointed fingernails into the prophet's hide. But what was one woman compared to the power of Jehovah, which he had just witnessed on the mountain? No comparison!

The great prophet was tired, hungry, and emotionally drained. All motivation killers. All triggers that make us feel as if we too have had enough. What does this say to us? Give yourself time to rest and revive your energy before you pull the plug on your dreams.

Elijah was singing the blues. He was singing his own swan song. Surely, as a good Hebrew man he would have known the words of David: "He put a new song in my mouth." [6] That's what that man of God needed—a fresh, uplifting melody streaming from his thought closet like the kind of song Deborah sang...

"March on, my soul, with courage!" [7]

How about you? What kind of song do you sing to your soul? What kind of melodies flow from your thought closet when you are discouraged? When the battle is raging, what do you sing? When you've been knocked down by circumstances, what do you sing? When you're standing on top of the mountain, what do you sing? My friend, the situations can vary, and they will, but the song must stay the same. You must speak and sing perseverance to your soul.

Richard Nixon, our nation's thirty-seventh president and a man who experienced his share of hard knocks, said, "Defeat does not finish a man, quitting does. A man is not finished when he's defeated. He's finished when he quits."

Your thought closet may be full of big mistake milestones and poorly sung words. You certainly have had and certainly will have times when you just want to get off the field and quit. Remind your soul to focus on the finish, not the flaws and failures.

One poorly sung note will often make you want to stomp off the field and swear off singing forever, but to you, my sisters, I say, *sing on.*

Someone else once put it this way: When your dreams turn to dust, vacuum!

Soul-Talk Questions to Ponder

1. What are your motivation killers?

2. Is your soul wrinkled?

3. Have you ever had an "Elijah episode"? If so, how can you prevent it from happening in the future?

4. Has one poorly sung note (one past mistake) kept you down, making it hard for you to persevere? If so, before you go on, stop and ask God to help you. He offers forgiveness, He empowers you to make restitution (if needed), and He restores and redeems all the lost years. Trust Him.

For more tips and resources to help you press on, go to MeMyselfandLies.us. There you'll find pictures of me from my big-hair days singing the national anthem and some songs that have helped me keep marching on!

Passages to Ponder

But we're not quitters who lose out. Oh, no! We'll stay with it and survive, trusting all the way (Hebrews 10:39 MSG).

Not only so, but we also rejoice in our sufferings, because we know that suffering produces perseverance; perseverance, character; and character, hope (Romans 5:3-4).

May the Lord direct your hearts into God's love and Christ's perseverance (2 Thessalonians 3:5).

Therefore, since we are surrounded by such a great cloud of witnesses, let us throw off everything that hinders and the sin that so easily entangles, and let us run with perseverance the race marked out for us (Hebrews 12:1).

You need to persevere so that when you have done the will of God, you will receive what he has promised (Hebrews 10:36).

But as for you, be strong and do not give up, for your work will be rewarded (2 Chronicles 15:7).

Finally, be strong in the Lord and in his mighty power (Ephesians 6:10).

A SNEAK PEEK INTO MEREDITH ANDREWS'S THOUGHT CLOSET

After getting to know this bright and tender singer/songwriter, I understand why *Billboard* magazine chose Meredith as one of their "Faces to Watch." She is worth watching. As a young mom of three, she hit a rough patch in her life and marriage, and she knows what it's like to fight feelings of failure and just want to plain quit! But I've watched her march on anyway! You'll be inspired by her practical perseverance.

"The thing I wrestle with the most is the nagging feeling that I'm failing those around me. Wearing so many hats and juggling responsibilities is always tricky, and I constantly feel the tension between family and ministry. I've felt spread so thin—like I'm not doing anything well. And it used to be on a weekly basis. Things began to change for me though when I got honest about what I was giving my yes to, and being willing to say no to good things in order to say yes to what was best. I used to say yes to anything and everything, mostly because I didn't want to let anyone down. My family was getting my leftovers. I was completely overwhelmed by my schedule and didn't know how to rest. Yet God isn't looking for us to wear ourselves ragged. Our culture applauds striving and straining while God's economy looks more like faith and rest. I want to live from that place.

"When I begin to feel like a failure, I go back to two fundamentals. First, God's promise. The promises of God are true for all of time. If He has called me to something, promising that He would equip me to do it, then it's going to happen no matter my feelings of failure. I spend time reading the promises of God's Word and meditating on those encounters and moments where the voice of God spoke to my spirit with His call. The second thing I examine is my motives. Maybe I have been working hard at something I'm called to do, but somewhere along the way my motives may have been skewed through the pressures and obstacles of daily grinding it out. I ask God to return my heart to His purposes. All I can do is set my boat in the water; God has to put the wind in the sails!"

I grow stronger when I lift up God.

11

LIFT UP

PRAISE THE LORD, O MY SOUL

I could hear Brandon sigh from across the room.

"It's hard to make flamingos happy."

"Yeah," consoled Clayton, "I know."

Flamingos? I had just placed a large pizza on the table before my son and his friend. "How do you know about the emotional state of flamingos?" I asked.

Brandon began to explain that with his computer game, Zoo Tycoon, he could create natural habitats for animals. He ticked off a quick list of the animals that were easy to satisfy because their habitat needs weren't very complex.

"See, Mom," Clayton interrupted, "I *told* you computer games were educational."

"Flamingos," Brandon went on, "are never satisfied with their habitat."

"Really?" I asked. "So what kind of habitat do these persnickety birds require?"

The guys went on to talk about the balance between salt water and fresh water. They described the exact amounts of sand and savannah grass that flamingos craved.

I must admit, the boys had a lot better handle on the subject than I did. When I think of flamingos, they're usually hot pink and plastic, sticking out of a summer drink or planted in someone's yard. The boys continued to formulate how they could make those flamingos happy.

I sank my teeth into my slice of pizza and thought, *Maybe it's hard to make flamingos happy because they're a lot like people.*

We humans are a persnickety flock too. If life doesn't present just the right balance, or if our habitat falls a bit below our standards, we tend to puff out our feathers in indignation. Some of us seem to share the attitude of those pink-feathered friends of ours. We think that happiness is simply a matter of habitat, and if we could somehow adjust all of the happenings of a given day, we would be happy.

In other words, if we could make it well with our circumstances, it would be well with our souls. The fact is, happiness really has very little to do with our habitat. But it has everything to do with our hearts.

Heart Exam

"Twelve minutes," the technician said as I stepped on the tread-mill for my stress test.

"What? Do you mean I need to walk for twelve minutes?" I asked.

"No," she said. "Actually, I was letting you know today's record." She seemed deliberate about awakening my competitive nature, bragging on the prowess of the 52-year-old man who treaded just before me.

If that was a scheme to get me moving, it worked. I was certainly not going to let a 52-year-old guy beat a 42-year-old woman! Stepping up onto the treadmill, I focused on pacing myself into first place, even if I had to pant and sweat every step of the way.

When the tech realized I was preparing to win the race of a life-time, she quickly backpedaled. "Whoa! I want you to push yourself, but don't go crazy here! Remember, you're doing this because of an abnormal EKG, so be wise."

Yes, I was covered with sticky little wires and dressed in a fashionable hospital gown because my last checkup revealed some irregularities in my heart. It had something to do with bundles being blocked and signals getting stuck.

I really have no idea what all of that was about. But I do know the doctor said I was probably born this way. Even though something seemed irregular on the test, it was all very regular for me!

So I wasn't concerned. I just shaved my legs, slipped on my Nikes, and got ready to run, run, run.

The pace on the treadmill was leisurely at first, like a stroll around a lake or a meander in the mall. But as the minutes passed, that moving belt quickened and the incline increased. It became more difficult for me to keep up. But I still had four minutes before I could break the record, so faster and higher I went!

A *hooray* erupted from the two technicians who monitored my test and laughed at my tenacity. Twelve minutes and 15 seconds! I heard the victory chant, imagined the wind in my face as I broke through the finish-line ribbon, and jumped off the machine.

But it wasn't over.

Immediately, they maneuvered me over to a table for a sonogram of my chest. I only had a few seconds for this because they wanted to examine my heart while it was still racing.

So now I was lying on the table, submitting to the next part of the exam. I can't say I felt terribly comfortable about it. As you probably know, in these settings one is not fully clothed, and an awkward professional intimacy occurs between the patient and the health care provider.

So there I was, sweating and panting, parts of me being tugged and maneuvered as she completed her test.

Just then, out of the blue, she asked, "Do you really know Beth Moore?"

What did she say? I thought. *Am I hallucinating? Is this what happens when you've sent too much oxygen to your brain?*

I asked her to repeat what she had said.

"Oh," she replied, "I read your book *Lessons I Learned in the Dark,* and I saw that Beth Moore wrote the foreword. I just love Beth Moore!"

I told her that I loved Beth too.

But then I thought, *Wait a minute…she's read my book, and all she can talk about is the Beth Moore foreword? Why didn't she say, "I just love your book"?* Suddenly, lying there in my lovely gown, sweat dripping from every inch of my tired flabby body, I began to laugh.

Of all the places that I would prefer *not* to be recognized as an author, this would top the list. And then, when someone actually did recognize me, I was disappointed because it wasn't all about me!

I had a heart irregularity all right. But the real problem wasn't the blocked bundles and stuck signals the doctor had been concerned about. The deeper issue with my heart was that it was deeply self-centered—focused on lifting up myself.

Healthy hearts are centered on others, not on self. And a healthy heart is a happy heart.

Helen Keller once wrote, "Many people have a wrong idea of what constitutes true happiness. It is not attained through self-gratification, but through fidelity to a worthy purpose." To know that those words came from a woman who never saw and never heard, whose "habitat" was silent and dark, make them deeply profound and worthy of our attention.

Helen Keller said that happiness comes from fidelity or loyalty, from devotion to a worthy purpose. So think about it. What do you consider a worthy purpose? Yes, I know that many of the expected sort of answers come quickly to mind: fighting poverty, promoting political issues, stamping out illiteracy, maintaining religious fervor. Those are certainly worthy purposes, but try to go a little deeper.

Open the door of your thought closet and look inside. What consumes your thoughts? When you have an idle moment, where do your thoughts wander? When you talk to yourself, what are you usually saying?

Even a little of this kind of questioning will help you determine what you consider a worthy purpose. It's really all about what you're already devoted to.

The purposes that drive your life *already* fill your thought closet. You can track them by the space they take up on your calendar, by the phone log of your cell phone, by the outbox on your e-mail, by your Internet surfing history, by last month's credit card statement, or by your check register.

Chances are, what you are loyal to has a lot to do with you— your dreams, your needs, your expectations, your life, your past, your relationships, your weight, your hobbies…you, you, you, and you!

All of that self-focus on our own well-being, however, doesn't really make us happy. In fact, it has the very opposite effect. Like restless flamingos, we're never quite satisfied with our habitat. Ruffled feathers tell the unhappy story of our lives.

Other Centered

At a large arena speaking event, I entered the catering room with my assistant for lunch.

"Hi, Jennifer!" I recognized a cheery voice. It was Pat, already seated with her meal at a table.

"Pat," I said, "you're the first one here. How did you get in here so fast?"

With delicious irony and a sassy lilt to her voice she said, "Well, I had to hurry to get here before all the selfish people!"

Her quip gave me a good laugh, but it was also a timely reminder. Easily mindful of other people's selfishness, we're often blind to our own. If you told your soul to tune in (chapter 5), you're probably already alert to your own tendency toward selfishness. It's our nature.

As babies we cry when our needs aren't met. In childhood, we get in trouble for not sharing our toys. During the teenage years, we imagine we're the only ones people see when we enter a room. By the time we reach adulthood, we ought to be a little more aware of our self-centered tendencies.

If not, getting married clues us in. If that doesn't do it, having children exposes any remaining selfishness!

It's just our nature to lift ourselves up, to be egocentric. Looking back at my life (and sometimes I don't have to look back far), I can say for sure that the most miserable times of my life have been when I was the most self-centered, self-absorbed, and self-promoting. Those were the times when I told myself, *It's all about me.*

I tell my boys, "Selfish people aren't happy people." That's a good thing to talk to myself about too.

When we tell our souls to get the spotlight off our own preoccupations and onto the needs of others, we reopen the potential for joy in our lives—joy that we may have thought we'd never experience again.

At the same time, let's not confuse selflessness with lack of self-regard. Selflessness involves a true understanding and appreciation of self. Actually, when you know who you are and are secure in your identity, you have a healthy foundation from which selflessness can blossom.

Only selfless, other-centered people are truly happy. They have learned the all-important key. When we lift others up, we grow stronger, healthier, and happier.

Who knew this better than Mother Teresa? An Albanian-born humanitarian and missionary, she gave her life away to the poor and forgotten. "Like Jesus," she said, "we belong to the world, living not for ourselves but for others."

Her treasure trove of wisdom includes many worthy truths.

She wrote, "I have found the paradox, that if you love until it hurts, there can be no more hurt, only more love." Building on that thought, she added, "A sacrifice to be real must cost, must hurt, must empty ourselves."

The most perfect portrait of selflessness is Christ. He demonstrated His other-centeredness by His willing choice to empty Himself, laying aside all claims to what was rightfully His. When we are truly selfless, we do the same. Like Mother Teresa, we are willing to set aside our rights and to pour ourselves out, to empty ourselves for others.

> Do nothing from selfishness or empty conceit, but with humility of mind regard one another as more important than yourselves; do not merely look out for your own personal interest, but also for the interests of others (Philippians 2:3-4 NASB).

That is the example of Christ, and any flamingo that follows along that path will be among the happiest birds on the planet.

Giving of ourselves keeps us connected to God's creativity and compassion. It also allows us to live out God's intention that we would be connected with each other, a human community of support and love. As Jesus put it, that we may be one, just as Christ and the Father are one.

The polar opposite of selflessness is selfishness, best captured in the phrase "It's all about me." Ironically, that kind of self-centered approach is actually a sign of identity confusion. It's a symptom of not understanding your true value and purpose. When you recognize your secure position in God, you are able to risk granting attention to others and giving them praise.

Here's the irony: What can appear on the surface to be an inflated opinion of self is often a flimsy attempt to compensate for the very opposite.

Check out these symptoms. They will help you know if you are in the lonely center of your thought closet.

- The cashier at the grocery store doesn't make eye contact. Instead of feeling compassion for her (she might be having a bad day), you think she's rude—or just doesn't like you.

- The doctor's office doesn't return your call promptly. You think it's because he doesn't value you as highly as his other *more important* patients. His tardiness has nothing to do with the fact that he may be busy or have an emergency.

- Someone cuts you off in traffic. Rather than recognizing that we all make mistakes or sometimes act inappropriately, you respond, "What? Do you think I'm invisible!"

- No one at the party initiates conversation with you. You think people should approach you and ask, "How are you?" The idea that you should make the effort to do the same just never occurs to you.

- Your spouse says, "Somebody left the milk out." You spout, "It wasn't me. You're always blaming me!" You don't notice that you were not the target of the comment.

So here are warning signs for an out-of-balance self-awareness:

- If you crumble at criticism, your skin is too thin!

- If you are overly offended by people's behavior, you might just have an inflated view of yourself.

- If you take personally every comment made in your presence, chances are you think the world revolves around you!

Any of these is evidence that you aren't living out the identity you long for.

So what are you doing sitting in the middle of your thought

closet? It could get a little cramped and stuffy in there! Make room for thoughts of others on those shelves. Here are some ways to help your soul refocus on others.

- Pray that you will decrease and God will increase. Ask for direction in your life to do God's will. Remember God's will for Christ was to give until it hurt, to become poor so we could be rich, and to die so we could live.

- Practice emptying yourself. Give yourself a time-out to focus on others—their needs, their situations, and their desires.

- Stay connected. Recognize the importance of relationships and being available to others. Remaining self-centered is easier if you remain isolated. (In other words, flamingos that flock together forget to be so picky about the details of their habitat!)

The Great Other

When we tell our souls to lift up others, we find our own spirits are lifted to happier places. If I give someone else a boost, I find that I've climbed higher too. But there is One whom we cannot neglect telling our souls to lift up. He is the Great Other.

C.S. Lewis wrote, "From the moment a creature becomes aware of God as God and of itself as self, the terrible alternative of choosing God or self for the centre is opened to it."

Instead of indulging in self-exaltation, which leads to frustration and unmet expectations, lift up God. As He grows bigger in your thought closet, you grow smaller. This makes more room for others and will bring you true satisfaction. The psalmist told his soul to lift up God: "Praise the LORD, O my soul; all my inmost being, praise his holy name." [1]

We begin to fully enjoy God when we tell our souls to lift Him up, to praise Him. When we fully enjoy God, we can't help but praise Him. When He becomes the center of our attention, we no longer take that spot.

This positions us for true happiness. "God does not die on the day when we cease to believe in a personal deity, but we die on the day when our lives cease to be illuminated by the steady radiance, renewed daily, of a wonder, the source of which is beyond all reason."

I love that quote above from Dag Hammarskjold. When we lift up God, we open the door of our inmost being to that warm, steady, beautiful radiance. Lift up the Lord, honor His name, give Him praise, sing in concert with the angels, and a little bit of heaven rubs off on you.

> Rejoice in the LORD, O you righteous!
> For praise from the upright is beautiful (Psalm 33:1 NKJV).

You may think you have the door to your thought closet locked, bolted, and secured. But you really can't hide what fills those shelves. The contents sneak out with our thoughts and perceptions, seeping out into daily conversations. The writer of Proverbs said it this way: "Keep your heart with all vigilance; for from it flow the springs of life." [2]

How happy we are when God is in the center of our thoughts, our hearts. As a result, love for Him becomes a part of all we do and say, all we think and perceive. And everyone around us knows it!

That's why lifting up God is not reserved for a sanctuary. Praise is an overflow of what's in our thought closets. If you love something, you can't help but talk about it, right?

I overheard some women in my local coffee shop talking about their Christmas holidays.

"All he talked about was how he redid the basement!" one woman moaned about her brother. "He showed before and after photos and made us all watch the video of him doing the drywall! He even brought out blades from the new table saw he bought! It was painful!" she concluded.

"He can't help it; he just enjoys what he does," consoled her friend.

In *Reflections on the Psalms,* C.S. Lewis says, "I think we delight to praise what we enjoy because the praise not merely expresses but completes the enjoyment; it is its appointed consummation."

Praise is part of enjoying anything—coffee, pastries, flowers, sunsets, books, home-improvement projects, or anything else you might be into. To enjoy something fully, you must talk about it! The same applies to God. To enjoy Him fully, you must speak of Him. You must talk about Him.

You must think about Him. You must lift Him up. To really begin enjoying God, He must take up lots of room in your thought closet. The more room He takes up, the less room in your thought closet you consume! And believe me, this makes for a much happier soul.

The catechism of the Church of Scotland says that "man's chief end is to enjoy God and to praise Him forever." What I love most about that statement is that enjoying God and praising Him are really one and the same. In other words, enjoyment equals praise, and praise equals enjoyment! When God calls us to praise Him, He is calling for us to enjoy Him and His benefits. As we center our souls on God, we lose ourselves in His wonder.

Just listen to David as he describes a moment of true worship. He seems to be unable to string together words strong enough or bright enough to express himself!

> How priceless is your unfailing love!
> Both high and low among men
> find refuge in the shadow of your wings.
> They feast on the abundance of your house;
> you give them drink from your river of delights.
> For with you is the fountain of life;
> in your light we see light (Psalm 36:7-9).

By lifting up the Lord, David lifted himself into a place of radiance, delight, and joy.

Conversely, when we shut the doors of our thought closets to the God who loves us, we are most cruel to our own souls. Lifting up self barricades us from true happiness. Ironically, our own selfishness deprives us from what we long for most.

When we lift up others we grow smaller. And ultimately, as we lift up God, we find unlimited satisfaction in our own lowliness.

"As long as you are proud," C.S. Lewis wrote, "you cannot know God. A proud man is always looking down on things and people; and, of course, as long as you are looking down, you cannot see something that is above you."

When we lift Him up instead of ourselves, we're looking up instead of down. We're wrapping ourselves in the wonder of all that He is.

How much better is that? There's no comparison!

The Bible tells us that God takes pleasure in our praise. But when we set aside worries about our habitats and lose ourselves in the life-shaping, darkness-chasing, happiness-enhancing experience of pure praise, the pleasure is all ours. Ah, it *is* well with our souls.

Soul-Talk Questions to Ponder

1. Who or what is in the center of your thought closet?

2. When you're feeling painfully self-aware, what might you tell yourself about the focus of your attention?

3. After doing some careful soul searching, what are you devoted to? Is it a worthy purpose?

For more tips and resources to help you lift up, go to MeMyselfandLies.us. You'll also find my favorite quotes on lifting up God and others and some fun pictures of me and Beth Moore (and yes, the foreword that the health tech loved so much!).

Passages to Ponder

You will make known to me the path of life;
In Your presence is fullness of joy;
In Your right hand there are pleasures forever
(Psalm 16:11 NASB).

Let the words of my mouth and the meditations of my
heart be acceptable in your sight, O LORD
(Psalm 19:14 NASB).

Happy are those whose greatest desire is to do what
God requires; God will satisfy them fully!
(Matthew 5:6 GNT).

I will praise the LORD, who counsels me;
even at night my heart instructs me (Psalm 16:7).

In God we make our boast all day long,
and we will praise your name forever (Psalm 44:8).

He must increase, but I must decrease (John 3:30 NASB).

A SNEAK PEEK INTO LISA WHELCHEL'S THOUGHT CLOSET

My friend Lisa is an actor, speaker, and author of several books including the massively popular *Creative Correction*. She grew up playing Blair on *The Facts of Life* and as a grown-up, she was featured on *Survivor: Philippines*. She's in lots of Hallmark movies and is just so talented. But even though she is often center-stage, she's learned to remember God first in her thoughts and make Him the center of her thought closet. She's one actor who no longer rehearses her conversations or accomplishments.

"I've had imaginary dialogues in my head, between me and people whose approval I seek—the Lord has really asked me to stop having those conversations. If I want to talk about them, He asks me to turn them into prayer, a conversation with Him. I feel I can do that with Him. I can rest in the safety of how He feels about me enough to not be perfect. I think with other people, and even with myself, I want to be perfect, and I will make sure I have rehearsed or thought through everything I said or want to say so that I can give that appearance. But with the Lord, I don't feel that need. I don't have to have it all together. It really has been awareness of those inner conversations that has helped me take my thoughts to the Lord as prayers."

APPENDIX 1

SOUL-TALK STARTERS

Here's some truth to tuck away in your thought closet.

I am gifted with power, love, and a sound mind (2 Timothy 1:7).

I am chosen for success (John 15:16).

I am complete (Colossians 2:9-10).

I am secure (Romans 8:31-39).

I am confident (Philippians 1:6).

I am free (Romans 6:16-18; 8:1-2).

I am capable (Philippians 4:13).

I am spiritually alive (Ephesians 2:5).

I am God's workmanship (Ephesians 2:10).

I am welcome in God's presence (Ephesians 2:18; Hebrews 4:14-16).

I am sheltered and protected in God (Colossians 3:3).

I am valuable to God (1 Corinthians 6:20).

I am a member of God's family (Ephesians 2:19; 1 John 3:1-2).

I am God's treasure (1 Peter 2:9-10).

I am dearly loved (Colossians 3:12).

I am being transformed (2 Corinthians 3:18).

I am a new creation (2 Corinthians 5:17).

I am forgiven (Ephesians 1:6-8).

I am an heir of God (Romans 8:17).

I am a friend of God (John 15:15).

APPENDIX 2
HOW TO MAKE IT WELL WITH YOUR SOUL

My friend,

I don't want to introduce you to a religion; I want you to experience a relationship like the one that's changed my life.

When I transferred my trust from me to Christ, it became well, once and for all, with my soul. And the same can happen for you, my friend.

God loves you. He created you to know and love Him. But human beings sin, and that separates us from God. He is perfect, but we're not, so we can't know Him intimately and go to heaven to be with Him when we die.

Heaven is also perfect, so only perfection can dwell there. God knew we wouldn't be perfect like Him, and still He loves us and wants us to know Him and be with Him. How can we bridge the gap? What can we do to get rid of our sin so we can be right with God?

Try hard to be good? How good is good enough?

Volunteer? How do we know if it's enough?

Go to church? How often?

Keep the Ten Commandments? What if you break one?

Here's the truth. Regardless of how good you are, you aren't perfect enough for heaven. There is one answer, one way to God, one remedy for your sin, one way to heaven: Jesus Christ.

About 2000 years ago, God made a way for you and me to go to heaven. He sent His only Son Jesus Christ to die (to receive the wages, take the punishment, and pay the debt) for our sins.

Believe and receive. Trust that Jesus is who He says He is and that what He did on the cross is enough—He died your death so you can live a life with God.

Ask God to forgive you for your sins, and ask Jesus to be your Savior. He will come into your life and make it well with your soul.

My friend, please consider these things. If I am wrong, I still lose nothing in the long run, for I have lived a life of deep satisfaction and meaning. But if I am right, I have gained everything, and I want the same for you.

If you want to enter into relationship with Christ, you can ask Him to be your Savior and Lord by praying a prayer like this:

Lord Jesus, I believe You are the Son of God. Thank You for loving me and dying on the cross for my sins. Please forgive me and give me the gift of eternal life. I ask You into my life and heart to be my Lord and Savior. Your presence in my life will truly make it well with my soul.

If you prayed that prayer, please let me know at:
www.jenniferrothschild.com
I can't wait to celebrate with you!

Jennifer

NOTES

Chapter 1—Not So Well with My Soul

1. See, for example, Joe Kolezynski, "Belief, Self Talk, and Performance Enhancement," *Selfhelp Magazine,* ww.selfhelpmagazine.com/articles/sports/selftalk.html.

Chapter 3—Choosing Wise Words

1. Proverbs 9:10; see also Proverbs 15:33
2. Proverbs 13:10 (NASB); see also Proverbs 10:8; 12:15
3. Proverbs 16:16
4. Proverbs 18:4
5. Proverbs 12:18
6. Proverbs 2:10
7. Proverbs 16:21 (NASB)
8. Proverbs 3:35
9. Proverbs 24:14
10. Proverbs 14:8 (NASB)
11. Proverbs 14:3
12. Proverbs 24:5
13. Proverbs 19:8

Chapter 4—Speaking Truth to Your Issues

1. Matthew 9:21 (Willams New Testament)

Chapter 5—Tune In

1. 2 Corinthians 5:17 (NLT)
2. C.S. Lewis, "A Note on Jane Austen," *Selected Literary Essays,* ed. Walter Hooper (Cambridge: Cambridge University Press, 1979), 178.
3. Romans 8:37
4. Isaiah 40:28-31
5. Romans 8:31-32 NLT
6. Romans 8:35
7. Romans 8:38-39
8. 2 Corinthians 1:3-4
9. Psalm 145:18-19
10. Isaiah 43:1
11. Jeremiah 32:17 NLT
12. Philippians 4:6-7 NLT
13. John 14:1
14. John 14:27
15. 2 Timothy 1:7

Chapter 6—Look Up

1. Isaiah 50:2; 59:1
2. Stanislaw J. Lec, *Unkempt Thoughts* (London: Minerva Press, 1967), n.p.

Chapter 7—Calm Down

1. James 4:1
2. Proverbs 15:1
3. Proverbs 19:11 NASB
4. Romans 5:1-2

Chapter 8—Look Back

1. C.S. Lewis, "Myth Became Fact," *God in the Dock* (Grand Rapids: Eerdmans, 1970), 66.

Chapter 9—Chill Out

1. Rob Schwarzwalder, "Slice of Infinity," *The Lion's Share,* August 10, 2006.

2. Ecclesiastes 4:6 esv

3. Ayala Pines and Elliott Aronson, *Burnout: From Tedium to Personal Growth* (Parsippany, NJ: Free Press, 1981), n.p.

4. Psalm 131:2 nasb

5. Revelation 4:3

6. Genesis 1:5,8,13,19,23,31

7. Psalm 23:2

8. Matthew 11:28

9. Peter Lyman, et al., "How Much Information? 2003." Available online at www2.sims.berkeley.edu/research/projects/how-much-info-2003/.

Chapter 10—Press On

1. Philippians 4:13 nasb

2. Hebrews 10:39

3. Exodus 14:13 nkjv; 14:15

4. Proverbs 24:33-34 nlt

5. 1 Kings 19:4

6. Psalm 40:3

7. Judges 5:21 nlt

Chapter 11—Lift Up

1. Psalm 103:1

2. Proverbs 4:23 rsv

LET'S KEEP TALKING...

I want you to know I've prayed God would allow this book to get into your hands at just the right time—when you need it the most. My deepest desire is that you find real freedom by applying the principles found in *Me, Myself, & Lies*. Speaking truth to my soul has helped me make it well with my soul...every day.

I don't know you by name, but I would love to. It would mean so much to keep in touch, to hear your story, and to know what meant the most to you. If you visit my website below, we can stay connected through my blog and through my email newsletter called *Java with Jennifer*. And if you've ever wanted to talk with a sophisticated tone, my computer will read aloud your e-mail to me...with a stylish British accent.

Meanwhile, my prayer for you is this:

> May God himself, the God of peace, sanctify you through and through. May your whole spirit, soul and body be kept blameless at the coming of our Lord Jesus Christ. The one who calls you is faithful and he will do it (1 Thessalonians 5:23-24 NIV).

Blessings,

Jennifer

visit **www.JenniferRothschild.com**
or write to
Jennifer Rothschild
4319 S National Avenue, Suite 303
Springfield, MO 65810

ME, MYSELF, AND LIES FOR YOUNG WOMEN

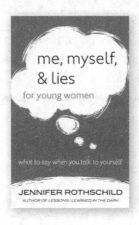

You've enjoyed being out with your friends, but on the way home, you suddenly start thinking...

I bet they don't like me...I wish I were more like them...I am such a loser!

Not for the first time, crazy phrases like these swirl in your mind and pool deep in your heart. How can you stop the negative thoughts and find some peace? Popular author and speaker Jennifer Rothschild shows you how to...

- *chill out* by letting your soul rest in God
- *look up* and let Him fill you with hope every day
- *press on* by finding the strength you need to get through tough times

Learn how to turn off the lies and listen to God's truth about who you are and all He has planned for you.

To learn more about Harvest House books and
to read sample chapters, visit our website:

www.harvesthousepublishers.com

HARVEST HOUSE PUBLISHERS
EUGENE, OREGON